ANSWERS

From

<u>EXPERTS</u>

On Selling a Home

Sage Advice from 18 Top-Selling
Real Estate Agents in North America

Aaron Kinn	Adrian Petrila
Amy Coleman	Bob Zachmeier
Bruce Hammer	Chase Horner
Dawn McCurdy	Frank Profeta
Igor Krasnoperov	Joey Trombley
Kimberlee Canducci	Len T. Wong
Lester Cox	Lynn Horner Baker
Michael Lewis	Paul Rushforth
Warren Flax	Willie Miranda

Out of the Box Books
Tucson, Arizona

ISBN: 978-0-9801855-3-9

Visit the publisher's website at:
www.outoftheboxbooks.com

When it comes to books… think Out of the Box!

Out of the Box Books
P.O. Box 64878
Tucson, AZ 85728

Table of Contents

Table of Contents

INTRODUCTION

This book will assist anyone, whether a novice or experienced veteran, to prepare, list, market, and sell their home. The authors have over **300 years** of combined experience and have collectively negotiated more than **35,000 home sales**.

The topics in this book are arranged in the order they would typically occur in a home sale. As you navigate the home-selling process, use this book to guide you.

Chapters 1-3 – Understanding the home-selling process

Chapters 4-6 – Preparing your home to show at its best

Chapters 7-9 – Choosing the right agent and marketing plan

Chapters 10-13 – Pricing strategies that net the most money

Chapters 14-16 – Calculating and adjusting to fit the market

Chapters 17-18 – Inspection and contract considerations

Knowledge arms you with a stronger negotiating position, enabling you to strike a better deal. This book will help you sell your home for the highest price in the shortest time while avoiding many of the mistakes made by other sellers and inexperienced real estate agents.

Enjoy!

1

Selling Fast For Top Dollar

Lester Cox
Pacific Arizona Real Estate
Tempe, Arizona

ANSWERS FROM EXPERTS ON SELLING A HOME

The first thing sellers must understand is *why* they are selling their home. Your motivation to sell is a determining factor in how to approach the process. It affects everything from the initial asking price to the amount of time, money and effort invested to prepare your home for sale. The list price is the number one determining factor on whether a home will sell and how fast. If you are in a declining market, it can be very dangerous and extremely costly to overprice your home, as you will be continually chasing the selling train down the tracks. In fact, if the market is declining in value at all, your home should be priced to be the very next home sold.

Although *you* know your reasons for selling, keep them to yourself, as they will affect the way the sale is negotiated and could give the buyer an advantage in the negotiation. For example, if the buyer learns that you must move quickly, you could be placed at a disadvantage in the negotiation. If asked about this information, it would be better to deflect the question by simply stating that your housing needs have changed. In truth, there is no need for anyone other than your real estate agent to know the reasons you are selling your home.

Because setting a price is such an important step in the process, sellers must do their homework before settling on a price. When the price is set, it will tell buyers that this is generally the absolute maximum that they will have to pay for the home. You will want to set a list price as close to the anticipated selling price as possible. If the price is too high, you run the risk of buyers and agents failing to take your home seriously. If the price is too low, you could end up handing over your property for a much lower price than might have otherwise been achieved through negotiation. The initial price is perhaps the most important step in ensuring the highest selling price for your home.

Many strategies can be used to estimate the price at which your home will sell, but they depend on the location of your home. If in a subdivision surrounded by other homes built in the same period with similar or identical floor plans, sellers can simply look at recent sales in the neighborhood. If the home is in an older neighborhood, the process gets a bit trickier. Because neighborhoods change over time, each home may be different in minor or even substantial ways, so it may be necessary to consult a professional real estate agent.

One useful method of determining your asking price is to put yourself in the position of the buyer by doing some "home shopping." Think of yourself as a buyer who is seeking out all available homes to find out what amenities they offer and how they are priced. If there are open houses in the neighborhood, check them out. If you are serious about getting your home sold fast, never price it higher than other homes in the neighborhood.

Sellers rarely benefit from getting an appraisal of their home. While the appraisal is a professional opinion of value and will demonstrate the fact that the home can be financed, the problem is that there are three types of appraisals and they all expire. The appraisal is unlikely to be of any use for the buyer. A good real estate agent is a better source for determining the value of your home. Once the home is under contract, there will be plenty of time for an appraisal, and the buyer will typically pay for it.

What do tax assessments mean? Some people think that they are a way of evaluating the value of a home, but there is a problem with that approach. The difficulty arises out of the tax assessment process itself: these assessments are based on criteria that may have little correlation to actual property values. Tax assessments are almost useless in determining the market value of a home.

When you decide to employ the services of a real-estate agent, it is important to choose the right one. According to the National Association of Realtors, nearly two-thirds of people surveyed who sold their home themselves said that they would not do it again. Some of the difficulties encountered when trying to sell on your own include price-setting, marketing, liability concerns, safety issues, and time constraints. When deciding on a real estate agent, choose a full-time, successful agent—not one who tells you what you want to hear with an inflated opinion on the value of your home.

All real estate agents are not the same. A top-performing agent knows the market and has information on properties for sale, past sales, and pending sales. A good agent will have a marketing plan, a solid presence on the Internet, and a supporting team of professionals. Sellers should also evaluate a potential real estate agent on their experience, qualifications, and enthusiasm.

Before settling on an asking price, give thought to the negotiating spread. Your real estate agent can tell you what the selling price to asking price ratio is averaging in the area. For example, if similar homes in the area sold for 97% of the asking price, that leaves 3% wiggle room in the pricing so the buyer can do some negotiating. In a successful sale, the buyer receives some concessions and the seller receives what they anticipated.

The look and feel of your home will generate a greater emotional response from buyers. Prospective buyers react to what they see, hear, feel and smell even though you may have priced the home to sell. There is an old real estate adage, "If you can *smell* it, you can't sell it." If there are any odors in your home, make sure that they are favorable, like fresh-baked bread or cookies. Because sense of smell in humans is so strongly linked with emotions and memories, this is one area of the home presentation where you can make a subtle, but powerful, impression on prospective buyers.

One of the biggest mistakes a seller can make is to rely solely on their own judgment. Don't be shy about seeking the honest opinions of others. Ask for objectivity in assessing both the merits and drawbacks of your home. A good agent can provide an objective opinion and offer advice about what should be done to make your property more marketable.

Make sure that your home is clear and uncluttered. Fix everything that can be fixed by oiling squeaky hinges, declaring war on dust, cleaning hand prints, switch covers, and walls. Cabinets and closets should be cleaned out and cracked windows or mirrors should be replaced. Tiles should be scrubbed to make sure all grout is clean.

For a home on the market, spring cleaning comes every week. It's important to remember that you are competing with older homes and brand new homes, so you should visit a few model homes and take notice of how clean and uncluttered they are. Aim to emulate the appearance of the model homes. Put away the knick-knacks and try to make visitors imagine the home as their own. Decorations should be neutral in color and style to add a simple warmth and character.

The importance of odors cannot be over-emphasized. Unpleasant odors can be an absolute deal-killer. Sellers live in their home and grow accustomed to its odors to the point where they no longer notice them, but prospective buyers will notice them immediately. If there are smokers in your home, thoroughly clean the house to rid it of any tobacco odor. There should be no more smoking in the home after that point, and no clue of smoking, such as ashtrays, should be left out for buyers to see. If you have pets, take every precaution to prevent them from creating stains and odors. Animal feces in the yard should be cleaned up on a daily basis.

Sellers must disclose everything, so be sure to ask your real estate agent in advance for any mandated disclosure statements so they can be filled out completely and truthfully. Full disclosure early in the process can help avoid disputes and hard feelings later on.

CHAPTER 1 – SELLING FAST FOR TOP DOLLAR

Obviously, attracting many prospective buyers will put you in a better position. This is why maximizing your home's marketability is so important. When there are multiple buyers, you are no longer forced to compete with a single buyer. Instead, you can reap the benefits of the buyers competing with each other—a "divide and conquer" strategy applied to the world of real estate.

When negotiating with a buyer, keep in mind that you are doing just that— negotiating. Remember to let go of the emotions you have invested in your home and conduct yourself in a business-like manner. Many sellers do not successfully keep their emotions in check, so those who are able to do this can gain a great advantage over other sellers.

While you should never reveal your reasons for selling, do your utmost to learn about the motivations of prospective buyers. The better you know the buyers, the easier it will be to gain an advantage in negotiations. Knowing what motivates the buyers allows you to control the pace and duration of the process, to negotiate more effectively, and puts you in a better position to bargain when armed with this information.

As a rule, buyers are looking to purchase the best available property for the lowest possible price, while sellers are trying to achieve the highest amount possible. Because buyers and sellers have conflicting goals, information becomes leverage. Important pieces of information to obtain about a buyer are the amount of mortgage they are qualified to obtain and how much they can afford as a down payment. If a buyer is offering a very low down payment, your agent should contact the buyer's agent to determine whether the buyer really has the ability to purchase your home. The financial situation of the prospective buyer will play a significant role in the nature of the negotiation, so look for opportunities to utilize this information to your advantage.

Quite often, buyers will specify a time when they would "like" to close on the house, but in reality this is actually the point at which they *need* to close. Knowledge of a buyer's compelling deadlines can provide yet another negotiating advantage for the seller.

Unless you can afford two monthly mortgage payments, you should wait to sign any deal on your next home until your current home is under contract. Otherwise, you may end up in a desperate position to sell your home as quickly as possible, to avoid the burden to making payments on two homes at once. This desperation, of course, gives enormous power to buyers and can drastically lower the selling price of your home.

In most cases, it is better to occupy your home during the selling process. Visually, rooms appear larger and warmer with furnishings. When occupied, a home's air temperature is usually at a comfortable level and generally, the home will be appear to be better cared for than a vacant home. Also, if the home is vacant, a buyer may suspect that you already have another home, leading them to believe that you are desperate to sell. In this situation, the buyer will make a lower than normal offer.

A staged home typically shows better and sells faster than a home that isn't staged. Ask your real estate agent if they can recommend any home staging consultants. The objective opinion of a decorating professional can be very helpful to home sellers.

It is best <u>not</u> to have a hard deadline by which your home must be sold. This can cause undo stress and can give buyers the idea that you are desperate to sell your home, which is a huge disadvantage during the negotiating process.

As previously mentioned, you must leave emotion at the door when entering the negotiating room. Although hard, this means never taking a low offer personally. You may have years of emotional investment in your home, but the buyer simply sees it as another house and is doing their utmost to get a good deal. Every offer, no matter how low it may appear, should be evaluated objectively.

Work with your agent to formulate a reasonable and acceptable counter offer. To start the process of making a counter offer, analyze the offered price, the size of the earnest money deposit, the closing date, the size of the down payment, and whether or not the buyer is making any special requests. These factors represent the starting point of negotiations.

The low offer that many sellers throw aside may be the one they end up having to accept if they fail to formulate a thoughtful counter offer and supply documentation that supports their position. If you feel that the buyer may not be qualified or that their offer is inadequate, it is a good idea to find out more about their ability to carry the mortgage on your home. It is wise to ask how the buyer arrived at the amount of their offer and to suggest that they compare that price with other homes for sale in the area.

The day you put your home on the market, you should begin reading a blank form of the contract that will be used to facilitate the sale of your home. This will eliminate a lot surprises and give you a huge head start when the time for negotiation arrives. When an offer is made, be prepared to ensure that all the terms, costs, and responsibilities are spelled out and accurate.

Obviously, it is important to avoid deviating from the terms of the contract. For example, if the buyer requests a move-in date that comes prior to the date of closing, be extremely cautious. Complying with this request could open the door for the buyer, once moved into your home, to find something they do not like and then refuse to close. If the buyer needs a reason for the denial of their request to occupy early, simply state that you have been advised against it. Even if you feel inclined to comply with the buyer's wishes, remember that there is no good time to take unwarranted risks that could cause the deal to fall through. If you are inclined to allow for this request and are not working with a real estate agent, seek legal advice first.

Your home will be new to the market only once, so don't waste the opportunity to gain momentum from the excitement of introducing the property to the market. You only have one chance to make a first impression.

<u>About The Author</u>

Lester Cox

Pacific Arizona Realty
5440 S Lakeshore #104
Tempe, AZ 85283

(480) 775-7700

lester@wesellaz.com

www.wesellaz.com

Lester Cox was born and raised in the mid-western part of the country, Kansas City, MO. His father was a respected businessman who passed along his strong work ethic and the belief that there is no ceiling on what is possible.

When he was 17, Lester relocated to Phoenix with his mother and younger sister after the death of his father. After high school, Lester attended Phoenix College and Arizona State University where he studied business. After serving four years in the United States Air Force, Lester entered the real estate arena where he has found great success for more than 40 years.

His experience includes residential sales, new home sales, commercial real estate, development, and home building. In 1995, he founded his own company and began building a real estate team in 2001. Lester has been responsible for over 5,000 successful transactions totaling more than a *billion dollars*.

He and his team consistently close 400 to 500+ transactions each year and Lester has received numerous awards and accolades as one of the top real estate agents in Arizona and the real estate industry.

Lester is active in his community, giving thousands of dollars each year to charities benefitting children, like Make-A-Wish Foundation and Boys and Girls Clubs of America. He serves on the Board of Directors for REO4Kids, National Association of Hispanic Real Estate Professionals, and is a founding member of three real estate mastermind groups.

Lester is also a professional real estate coach for the Craig Proctor coaching program and co-facilitator of the Diamond Mastermind Group. He is the Master Broker for Arizona for the National REO Brokers Association.

Lester and his wife Pat have been married for 37 years and both work in their real estate company. They reside in Chandler, Arizona, with their Boxer named Lindlee and a Papillion named Trixie. They enjoy spending time with their siblings, many nieces and nephews, and close friends.

2

The Top 10 Pitfalls to Avoid

Adrian Petrila
Realty Direct
Naples, Florida

Selling a home can be a stressful experience, particularly if you don't get the offers you are expecting, or if your home doesn't sell in a reasonable amount of time. By preparing ahead of time, home sellers can increase their odds of selling quickly and for the best price. With that in mind, this chapter will outline the top 10 pitfalls to avoid when trying to get the best price and the fastest sale of their home.

10. Ignoring Curb Appeal

Regardless of how appealing a home may be inside, if careful attention is not paid to the exterior of the home, particularly the front, then you may lose out on selling opportunities even before viewers have opened the front door. The curb appeal – how your home looks from the street – is extremely important. If your home doesn't look good on the outside, people won't come inside. Prior to listing your home:

- Remove debris, leaves, and equipment from the yard
- Mow the grass regularly to keep it neat and short
- Consider planting shrubs or flowers
- Prune back trees and bushes
- Repaint the exterior, door, and trim (if possible)
- Power wash the driveway and walkways
- Wash exterior windows
- Clean gutters

Most of these exterior changes are affordable and easy to do. Improving curb appeal can boost showing activity and increase your chances of receiving an offer.

9. Skipping Pre-Sale Home Inspection

Sellers who have lived in their home for several years may have familiarity blindness and be unaware of major problems with their home. These problems could cost thousands of dollars to repair and cause potential buyers to walk away. A home inspection prior to listing your home can identify major problems such as roof leaks, drainage issues, and foundation concerns which can be addressed before the home is put up for sale.

8. Putting Off Minor Repairs

Home sellers tend to overlook minor repairs that their home requires, as they focus their attention on major issues that need attention prior to selling. This presents a problem because potential buyers will notice the minor issues and automatically assume that there must be major maintenance issues as well. This assumption may cause hesitation in making an offer or could result in a significantly lower offer than expected.

Prior to listing your home, carefully inspect the following items and make the necessary repairs:

- Caulk around windows and doors
- Oil doors to prevent squeaking
- Patch wall holes
- Fix or replace leaky faucets
- Replace burned-out light bulbs
- Remove old or torn wallpaper
- Repair or replace damaged trim and baseboards

Basically, any repair that can enhance the look or feel of your home is a good idea, as long as it doesn't cost too much. The cost of some improvements can be offset with a higher selling price.

7. Settling for a Basic Clean

A clean home is much more attractive to home buyers. Plan to spend several days giving your home a thorough cleaning prior to listing it for sale. The list should include: steam cleaning carpets, washing walls, cleaning windows, brightening tile grout, and ensuring that any odors are removed. In the world of home selling, there is no such thing as "too clean." Don't settle for a basic cleaning, aim for a spotless home that will have great appeal to potential buyers.

6. Avoiding an Investment

When selling, many home owners are reluctant to put more money into their home, because they believe that the benefit isn't worth their investment of time and money. Many low-cost investments can greatly improve the appearance of a home and can more than pay for themselves by leading to a higher offer price with less time on the market. These items should be considered:

- Repainting bedrooms and living areas
- Replacing carpet with laminate or hardwood flooring
- Changing door knobs and hardware
- Updating old fixtures and faucets
- Adding plants to rooms
- Installing larger mirrors in bathrooms or bedrooms

Many of these enhancements cost very little and can be completed in a weekend, but when it comes to selling a home they can really pay off.

5. Keeping Clutter

Before listing your home, carefully evaluate each room to determine what needs to be removed or relocated. A streamlined, de-cluttered home feels more spacious and is much easier for buyers to visualize as their own. Each room should be thoroughly de-cluttered, including basements and closets. A de-cluttered home is more attractive and less distracting. Presenting your home in the best light will attract higher offers.

4. Multi-Tasking Rooms

Many homes have rooms that serve a double-duty: such as an office that doubles as a guest room or a family room that doubles as an exercise room. While this may work for the family who currently resides in the home, it may put off home buyers, as it may be difficult for them to see the room rather than the contents. Prior to selling, it is wise to restore each room to its original purpose, rather than trying to make the rooms into something they are not.

3. Rejecting Offers

Everyone has a different strategy when it comes to buying a home. Some buyers may make a very low initial offer. By carefully considering all offers and countering with a fair and reasonable amount, sellers are more likely to negotiate a price that suits them. Rejecting low offers without countering may put off the potential buyer, who will simply move on to the next home on their list. By taking the time to construct a reasonable counter-offer, sellers can determine whether the buyer is seriously considering their home, and whether there is a chance of reaching an agreement.

2. Self-Listing a Home

Some companies advocate the money one can save by "selling their own home," but fail to mention that self-listed properties often spend more time on the market, and don't sell for as much as professionally marketed homes. According to the National Association of Realtors® (www.realtor.org) "for sale by owner" (FSBO) homes averaged a sale price of $140,000 in 2010, while similar homes sold by a qualified real estate agent or broker sold for nearly $60,000 more.

Many real estate agents have years of experience in marketing homes. They've found exactly what works to sell homes and which marketing channels in order to get the best response. A good real estate agent or broker can:

- Provide tips to make your home more appealing
- Obtain volume discounts in local newspapers and utilize various websites to maximize exposure
- Conduct open houses and home tours to attract more potential buyers to your home
- Recommend contractors, inspectors, and other reputable professionals who are reasonably priced
- Ensure that all parts of the transaction are completed accurately and effectively to reduce legal liability
- Provide detailed market analysis and pricing recommendations based on experience, not emotion

Home sellers should carefully consider whether the short term savings from selling their home themselves will achieve their long-term goal of selling their home for the highest price in the shortest time. Many sellers who try to sell their home themselves have difficulty getting the price they want and find that it takes much longer than they expect. In most cases, using a qualified real estate agent or broker will prove to be a wise decision and a less stressful experience.

1. Pricing Too High or Too Low

Correctly pricing a home is a key element in attracting buyers and quality offers. A home priced too high will turn off most buyers. Many won't even bother to view your home because it is perceived to be over-priced or out of their price range. Nearly 90% of purchasing decisions are based on price.

Conversely, a home priced too low may cause buyers to believe that there is a major defect with the home, which will also cause them to stay away. Either way, if a home is not priced correctly, little can be done to get the buyers to come inside or pay more or less than they believe the home is worth.

A real estate agent can provide a detailed analysis of the home, as well as a history of what other homes in the area have sold for, so sellers can determine the best price at which to list their home.

These ten tips will enable you to present your home in the best possible light, and ensure that you have all the tools necessary to attract a great offer in the shortest amount of time.

About The Author

Adrian Petrila

Realty Direct
4500 Executive Drive #330
Naples, FL 34119

(239) 598-9393

apetrila@adrianpetrila.com

www.adrianpetrila.info

Adrian Petrila started his real estate career in 2002 and has been involved in residential sales, new home construction, vacant land, broker price opinions, and distressed sale properties. His career successes include receiving Craig Proctor's Quantum Leap Award, $1M GCI Award, completing over 15,000 broker valuations, selling 150-200 homes per year, and being the #1 real estate agent (out of more than 4,000 agents) in Naples, FL, from 2008-2011 by total homes sold.

After several years as an individual agent, Adrian began building his real estate team in 2006. In 2008, he opened his own brokerage. Today he is the owner of three Realty Direct franchise offices in southwest Florida with over 150 agents. He is also the founder and CEO of BPOGenius.com, a software company servicing real estate agents in the valuation industry.

Adrian is an active member of the National REO Brokers Association (NRBA), Diamond Mastermind Group, and REO4Kids. He supports children's charities including Make-A-Wish Foundation, Boys and Girls Club, and others.

3

What to Expect When Selling

Len T. Wong
Len T. Wong & Associates
Calgary, Alberta

ANSWERS FROM EXPERTS ON SELLING A HOME

When putting your home on the market, it is very important to understand the process so you can set accurate expectations. Being educated and having realistic expectations can enable you to achieve top-dollar for your home in a short amount of time, giving you the ability to proceed to the next phase with minimal stress, whether buying or building another home.

After more than twenty years in real estate, I've found that the marketing plan and services provided by a real estate agent are the biggest things that define them. A seller should never hire a real estate agent simply based on their commission — a real estate agent charges what the market allows. Some agents will offer their services at a low price in order to get more business, but they also discount what they do. A good real estate agent will conduct a market analysis using a comparison between your home, current listings, and recent sales of homes in the area over the past three to six months. Strategic pricing, an important step discussed later in this chapter, ties directly into this analysis. A real estate agent offering a suspiciously low commission probably hasn't performed such an analysis.

Sellers should hire a real estate agent based on their marketing plan and the services they provide. Though commissions are negotiable, the old adage, "you get what you pay for" holds true. Many real estate agents offer a very low commission by placing the property in a multiple listing system (MLS), installing a sign, and doing little else to sell the home. By contrast, a real estate agent with a good marketing plan and negotiation experience will typically sell your home quicker and at a higher price. This can result in thousands of dollars in your pocket, which easily covers the difference in cost between a full-service agent and the low-commission agent who doesn't provide the same services. Again, you get what you pay for!

The essential ingredients of a marketing plan are exposure and innovation. When properly implemented, they enable home owners to sell their home for top dollar in the least amount of time—doubly important in a falling market! Sellers should ask potential real estate agents what they will do to maximize the exposure for their home. Just as more fishing lines in the water catch more fish, more mediums of exposure will attract more buyers to your home.

Examples of exposure include advertisements placed in real estate or other magazines, print media such as a local newspaper's real estate section, or a local real estate newspaper. The Internet has revolutionized the real estate market, so advertisements must be placed on line as well. National Association of Realtors (NAR) statistics show that more than 80% of home buyers start their search online. Numerous websites feature homes for sale and the technology is constantly improving.

Buyers can now use search engines to find homes in specific areas, view virtual tours of homes, and use social media sites like Facebook, Kijiji, Twitter, and Craigslist to get information about homes. Clearly, the old-fashioned open house is not as effective as it once was. On average, only about one percent of homes sell due to an open house. Some traditional exposure methods like print media remain important as not all home buyers are computer-literate.

Besides using various mediums of exposure, a real estate agent should also use innovative methods. One innovative marketing method is the "Tour of Homes," which includes several homes in the same area. Each home stays open for about fifteen minutes, and buyers can come back to a home they like to compare it to others. This is a great way to show your home to several buyers without tying up an entire afternoon.

Another innovation is the "Guaranteed Sale" program. A guaranteed sale usually means that the real estate agent or one of their investors agrees to buy the home if it doesn't sell after a specific period of time. This program can give sellers a sense of the confidence a real estate agent has in selling their home at the price range in which it is listed. Few real estate agents have the confidence to offer this program, but it offers both buyers and sellers with a win-win deal.

Most buyers would prefer to sell their existing home before buying a new one to avoid the burden of two mortgage payments. The "Trade-up" program provides the buyer with a guarantee that if they buy a new home, but cannot sell their old home, the real estate agent and/or brokerage will buy it from them. This program is similar to the "Guaranteed Sale" program, but the real estate agent guarantees the sale of your buyer's home so they can buy yours.

CHAPTER 3 – WHAT TO EXPECT WHEN SELLING

In addition to their marketing plan, it is also important area to consider the services a real estate agent provides. Do they work as an individual, or as part of a team? It makes sense to hire a team rather than a single agent, as an individual agent can't leverage themselves like a team. A busy individual may not have the time for extra accommodations such as showing your home on short notice but a team typically has the flexibility to do this.

If you choose to work with a team, find out how many assistants the team has to handle daily tasks like listing the property, creating feature sheets, taking photographs, generating online advertisements, taking measurements, and handling telephone calls. These are all very important aspects of selling your home. Also, you should ask how often they provide feedback and how they will coordinate showings so you will know that you are getting value in return for the commission you are paying.

In addition to dealing with a real estate agent, sellers must also deal with their property. Buyers will be looking at the repairs and touch-ups your property needs, so don't let these issues have a negative impact on negotiations. Utilizing the services of painters, electricians, plumbers, and other professionals in advance will ensure that your home shows well and can result in a faster sale for a higher price. Professionally staging your home can highlight its features and finishing touches, give buyers the feeling that your home is well-kept, and ensure that each room is balanced and tastefully decorated. Whether furniture and decorations are added or deleted, the goal of staging is to enable potential buyers to see a spacious interior in which they can imagine their own furnishings.

To avoid unwanted surprises, Sellers should obtain an updated real property report. This is a survey of the property that shows the improvements that have been done within City compliance.

When your home is listed and ready to show, pricing enters the picture. To be competitive in today's market, a house must stand out as the best buy in the area. By looking at other homes for sale in the area, a seller can determine where they want to be in the pecking order. Most buyers shop based on price, so it is important to be priced as well or better than the competition, even if that means just a $100 difference. When a price is selected, the home is ready for input in the Multiple Listing Service (MLS).

After your home is listed, monitor the feedback received from buyers and agents. The showing activity is also important to monitor in order to determine whether your price is on target. If you are getting lots of showings but no offers - or worse yet, no showings - the problem is probably the price. If no offers are received in the first three or four weeks, take a look at the price, comparing your home to recent sales of similar properties during the time your home was listed.

Being strategic and pro-active with the price is important. Adjusting the price can often re-energize the listing if done soon enough. Buyers who initially saw your home but didn't make an offer may be lured back by a lower price, and the price reduction can attract new buyers as well. If after another three to four weeks there is still no offer, another price adjustment may be in order. An aggressive and pro-active seller must keep adjusting the price until their home is sold, especially in a slow or declining market.

When an offer is received, it is time to enter into negotiation with the buyer. This is an important process that should be guided by a real estate agent. If priced right, you should receive offers close to the asking price. Often, the longer it takes to sell your home, the less you will receive so it is important to price it right and make adjustments quickly if showing and offer activity are too low.

Sellers should ensure that they understand the purchase contract and are aware of its key points. The most negotiated item is price, which must be acceptable to both the buyer and seller. Earnest money deposits are also important. The higher the deposit, the more financial incentive the buyers have to stay in the deal. The date of possession is another consideration that must be agreeable to both parties. This date must be coordinated to allow a smooth transition from one resident to another.

Conditions and deadlines must also be negotiated. The two most common are home inspection and financing conditions. Home inspections are critical to thoroughly check a home before buying it. Again, the importance of repairs and touch-ups must be emphasized. Sellers never want the issue of repairs or replacements to have a negative affect on negotiations. Buyers must be totally satisfied with the home after inspecting it thoroughly. Since repair requests after an inspection change the terms of the original contract, they must be negotiated. Usually cosmetic items are not considered in the home inspection. A real estate agent can guide you through what types of requests are typical and allowable in your state or province.

Financing is another common condition on a purchase contract so ensure that buyers are pre-approved by a reputable lender before entering into a contract. Depending on the bank or lending institution, an appraiser may be sent to the property, or an appraisal may be done online.

Another major condition to consider before accepting an offer is whether the sale of your home is subject to the buyers selling their home. In this case, the sellers agree to the offer price and conditions and go through the entire process, leaving only the sale of the buyer's home. What makes this condition interesting is that the seller's home typically stays on the market.

In the event that another offer is received, the seller may negotiate with the second party and come to an agreement. The first party is offered a "first right of refusal," which gives them the freedom to nullify their offer and walk away or drop the contingency to sell their home. Another condition can be that the contract is subject to their lawyer's review. All of these conditions are negotiable at the time the offer is made and guidance from an experienced real estate agent is highly advised.

CHAPTER 3 – WHAT TO EXPECT WHEN SELLING

The last thing to consider are the various items that will be included in the purchase price, sometimes referred to as "chattel". Basic appliances such as a stove, range hood, dishwasher, and garage door opener may commonly be included, depending on your area. Window coverings, washing machines, clothes dryers and refrigerators may also be included. It may be typical for a washer and dryer to be included in the sale of a condominium or townhouse but not in a home sale. Obviously, both parties must agree to these items so each party gets what they expect.

Once the conditions are negotiated or waived by the buyer, the seller can start packing! From there, the real estate attorney or escrow company can help process the deal. Depending on local laws, a lawyer, title company, or the real estate agent will handle the various documents and tasks required during this final process, including title registrations, couriers, real property reports, and additional costs incurred in the transaction, known as disbursements.

As the possession date moves closer, it is important to stay in contact with your real estate agent to ensure that everything is proceeding smoothly. Sellers should provide notice of when they will be out of the home and make sure to leave the property in the same condition it was in when the buyers first saw it. Sellers should notify utility companies, banks, and other companies that they will no longer be living at their previous address, and provide a forwarding address for mail and deliveries.

On the possession date, the buyers and their real estate agent will typically walk through the home to physically inspect it to ensure that there are no problems. The buyer's funds are usually received prior to closing. If the funds are not received in time to close, the buyers may be subject to daily late fees and interest. When the funds have been received and the necessary documentation has been signed and recorded, all parties will be notified and the keys will be released to the new owners.

There is a lot of information to understand if you are going to sell your home. Sellers who have been well-educated by their real estate agent will know what to expect and thus will find the process exciting, enjoyable, and stress-free.

About The Author

Len T. Wong

Len T. Wong and Associates
#20, 2439 – 54th Avenue SW
Calgary, Alberta T3E 1M4

(403) 287-4888

lenwong@calgaryhomesearch.com

www.lenwong.com

Len T. Wong grew up in the Real Estate Business. His father, Len Wong Senior, was a successful real estate broker in Calgary during the 70's and 80's with extensive hotel and real estate development experience. Upon completing a Hotel Administration degree in Las Vegas, Nevada, Len followed in his father's footsteps by establishing a career in real estate appraisal, hotel and property management, and development. He served on the 1988 Olympic Organizing Committee and was involved in Corporate and International Olympic Housing for the Calgary Olympic Winter Games.

Len started his career as an assistant to one of the top agents in Calgary. During his 20+ years with RE/MAX he was consistently ranked in the Top 100 agents and in the Top 25 in Canada over the past 10 years. Len has received every top award that RE/MAX offers including the prestigious Circle of Legends Award. Len is ranked in the top ten on the Calgary Real Estate Board (5,500 members) for the most listings and units sold during the past 10 years.

After leaving RE/MAX, Len established his own business with his partner of 15 years, Laura O'Connell. They've grown from one assistant to five full-time Agent/Associates and 5 full-time Coordinators who are the "glue" of the operation. As one of the most recognized teams in the Calgary real estate market, they have sold more than one billion dollars of real estate. Len has been featured in various real estate magazines and television news programs over the years as the "go-to" real estate agent in the city.

Len credits his father for his experience and background and his wife, Iris for her support of his business goals over the past 25 years. Craig Proctor, a highly respected real estate coach was an instrumental influence as Len's personal mentor. Of the 25,000 agents in North America who Craig has coached, Len was selected to receive the Quantum Leap Award for the most exceptional gains achieved through the aggressive and systematic implementation of Craig's Quantum Leap System.

Len carries the same success to his personal life and is considered one of the top basketball referees in the Calgary area. He enjoys golfing, yoga and traveling. Len is outgoing and enjoys building relationships with the people he meets. His biggest satisfaction and reward in the real estate business is helping individuals, friends, and families make one of the biggest investments of their lives!

4

10 Tips For Selling Your Home

Frank Profeta
Homeside Realty Group
Bohemia, New York

ANSWERS FROM EXPERTS ON SELLING A HOME

After making the decision to sell your home, it is important to prepare for the sale. This chapter will detail some simple tips on what to do and what not to do to sell your home in the shortest possible time for the highest amount of money.

#1: Have Your Home Pre-Inspected

Most sellers wait for a potential buyer to get a home inspection, but that is too late and could end up costing you thousands of dollars. By having your home pre-inspected by a qualified engineer or a licensed home inspector, you will know up front whether repairs are necessary. Having this important information allows sellers to repair necessary items long before the buyer's inspector arrives. Most buyers tend to multiply the cost of repairs indicated in the home inspection report and sometimes attempt to renegotiate the purchase price. Having the inspection done in advance can save you a lot of cash later on. Sellers who attempt to save money on a pre-inspection are often blind-sided by expensive repairs.

#2: Paint

Homes that look dingy or have a radical color scheme do not make a good first impression on a buyer. The cost of neutralizing bold colors is money well-spent and gives rooms a fresh and clean appearance. If your home had a previous roof leak that was repaired, water spots on the ceiling should be painted over because buyers may think that your home has a "bad roof," when it fact it is leak-free and under warranty. Remember that many people automatically assume the worst-case scenario—especially home buyers.

#3: De-Clutter

If you have lived in your home for a good length of time, or are a "pack rat" who likes to save everything, now is the time to de-clutter. A cluttered home will feel small and confining to perspective buyers who must squeeze through narrow passage ways and move your stuff to view your home. Imagine yourself in the buyer's position and think about how you would see their home if their stuff was scattered everywhere. Buyers will remember your home as the "home with a lot of stuff," and possibly forget many of the positive features that were lost in the clutter. If your home is cluttered, get storage containers, or better yet, a storage unit to keep your stuff. This will help immensely to sell your home and will give you a head start on packing. You should also consider having a yard sale or donating items no longer needed.

#4: Clean

No one likes a dirty house, so a little soap and water can go a long way. Bathrooms need to be spotless, which means hair needs to be removed from the drains, mildew needs to be removed from the shower, and the toilet needs to be scrubbed. Any bathroom items that aren't used daily should be put in a box and stored in a closet. Kitchen countertops should be cleared off, with unused appliances put away in a closet or cabinet. Countertops should be free of stains, the sink should not contain dirty dishes, and the cook top shouldn't have any burned food. Make sure that carpets are clean and vacuumed. If you have pets or are a smoker, take extra steps to ensure that your home is free of any foul odors. A person's sense of smell is strongly tied to their memory, so offensive odors can cause a potential buyer to have a negative memory.

#5: Put Away the Pets

You may have wonderful pets, but should keep in mind that other people may be afraid of your animals, especially dogs. When buyers walk through a home and there is an intimidating or overly-friendly animal, all they will remember is the animal, especially if they are scared and have small children with them. Take Fido for a walk or let him out in the yard when potential buyers come to see your home.

#6: Remove Sentimental Fixtures

If you have a special family heirloom chandelier hanging over a dining room table, or anything else that you intend to take with you, the item should be taken down and replaced before you begin showing your home. Many buyers want what they can't have, so if they don't *see it*, they won't want it! Doing this in advance will avoid potential problems that could break a deal.

#7: Curb Appeal

You need to be honest with yourself about whether your home is inviting and looks good from the street. You may consider power washing the exterior, planting flowers, trimming the hedges, weeding, rolling up the garden hose, and keeping the grass neatly cut. If you have a dog, be sure to pick up all the "good luck" in the yard before any showings. There's nothing worse than a buyer or agent stepping in something unpleasant and tracking it all over your home unintentionally. If you are selling in the winter and snow has covered the ground, make sure the driveway and walkways are free of snow and ice to prevent an accidental injury.

#8: Hide Valuables

It is surprising how many homeowners leave jewelry and other valuables out in the open. You probably don't know the people who walk through your home and sadly, not everyone is honest. There have been instances where other agents allow buyers to walk through unattended and, as a result, valuables go missing. Be smart and hide your valuables.

#9: Be Available

In any market, especially a slow one, you never want to miss a showing opportunity. Your home should be available to show as often as possible. At times, it may be inconvenient, but if you are serious about selling your home, make an effort to be flexible.

#10: Price Aggressively

You are not the only one trying to sell a home. Therefore, you must be very objective when pricing your home. The price should be based on similarly styled homes that have sold within the past three to six months or are currently under contract. The price should be reviewed at least every 3-4 weeks and adjusted accordingly. Try to remove your sentimental attachment to your home and be as objective as possible. The price must be set below other homes offering more features or your home will sit on the market unsold. In a declining market, you need to aggressively lead the market, not follow it downward. In doing so, you will create demand and sell your home before its value drops further.

By applying these ten simple tips, you will sell your home fast and for top dollar.

About The Author

Frank Profeta

Homeside Realty
80 Orville Drive, Suite 100
Bohemia, NY 11716

(631) 289-5151

frank@frankprofeta.com

www.frankprofeta.com

Frank Profeta has been selling homes on Long Island, NY since August, 1991. In April, 1996, he started his own real estate company out of his bedroom in his parents' home. Currently, Frank is ranked in the Top 10 among more than 24,000 real estate professionals on Long Island.

Frank's philosophy at Homeside Realty differs from most other brokerages. He has a "pay it forward" mentality and believes it is imperative to give back to his local community through educating the cooperating brokers, agents, homebuyers, and investors.

Frank has formed a *team* of agents and support staff, rather than emulating traditional brokerages that focus on getting as many agents working for them as possible. He is very selective and chooses only the most talented people. They work together toward one common goal: selling their client's homes fast and for top dollar with the least amount of hassle.

5

Getting Your Home Market-Ready

Michael Lewis
Lewis Real Estate Group
Flower Mound, Texas

ANSWERS FROM EXPERTS ON SELLING A HOME

Every seller wants to get top dollar for their home, and wants it to be sold fast. It's not by accident that some sellers accomplish their goal while others do not. Some treat the selling process as daunting and hair-raising, while others approach it with a well thought out plan that is executed to perfection, sending buyers scrambling for their checkbooks. This chapter contains a step-by-step process that, if followed, will have buyers making irresistible offers on your home.

The first thing to do is put yourself in the buyer's shoes. The exterior view of a home, better known as "curb appeal," is where every buyer looks first. This is where you must start. Sidewalks should be cleared and neat and the yard should be manicured to perfection, with the trees and shrubs nicely trimmed. Flower beds should be cleaned out with bright colored flowers freshly planted and leaves picked up. Make sure that the paint is not peeling or faded and that the house number can be easily seen from the street. Replace any non-working lights outside and make the front door shine like a new car. If a buyer sees a poorly-maintained lawn, paint peeling, and broken windows, you are likely to lose them. One quick and easy thing to do is to get a new "welcome" mat. Remember, you will never get a second chance at a first impression.

The worst thing that could happen to the potential buyer is to be greeted by a foul odor when the door swings open. In order to prevent this from happening, make sure to take out the garbage, and pick up any pet waste. To show your home at its best, you need light and lots of it. The blinds should be open and lamps should be on for a welcoming glow.

Carpets should be spotless and old rugs thrown out. If your furniture is chipped, frayed, or looks worn, it should be removed. You are trying to create a warm and cozy feeling, not an atmosphere more suggestive of a college dorm. Consider making small touches, such as a drop of vanilla on a light bulb, to create an inviting aroma.

Many buyers will judge a home by the way that its kitchen is kept, especially the oven and stove. Appliances must be spotless and the sink clean—never leave dirty dishes in the sink. The countertops and cooking areas should be kept open and uncluttered, without small appliances scattered over them. Cabinets should be rubbed down with oil to bring out a lustrous shine. Anything that squeaks, drips or sticks should be repaired or replaced, as buyers often open cabinet doors and drawers. Make sure that cabinets are not stuffed to the gills. Go through the pantry, the refrigerator, and the freezer and toss unused items to help get rid of clutter.

After the kitchen, bedrooms are the most-looked-upon area of a home. The key to presenting the bedroom is to define the room by arranging the furniture, allowing buyers to see the true space of the room. In order to showcase closet size, take out any clothing or accessories that you do not absolutely need. Overstuffed closets make them appear too small. Bedrooms should look immaculate so don't be afraid to be anal about how clean the rooms look. Beds should be made, with clothes off the floor and closets spotless.

Bathrooms must also be attractive. Buyers love to snoop, especially in the bathroom where there is the potential for some particularly unappealing sights to turn them away. Make sure there are no toys in the bathtub, hair on the floor or in the sink, stains on the toilets, or grout on the faucets. Everything in the bathroom should be immaculate.

The living room and family room should offer an atmosphere of relaxation, fun and activity. If you are a "pack rat" this is not the place to leave your mail and the last six months of newspapers—these items should be stowed away. Obsolete items, like a stack of VCR tapes should not be visible to buyers. If your goal is to sell your home, take the time now to purge unneeded junk, it gives you a head start on packing.

You want people to look at your home, not your excess stuff. This advice is important because if everything looks cluttered, potential buyers will think the house doesn't have enough storage space. Even worse, if you are messy, buyers may think that your home hasn't been properly maintained. Don't let the buyer's imagination start running wild, keep their attention focused on the merits of your home.

The last piece of the puzzle is the garage, where convenience is the key. The perfect garage would feature room for two cars and a well-organized work bench with an orderly storage area. This is not the place to dump the items cleaned out of the house. The garage also needs to look clean and uncluttered. If you have nowhere to store your things, consider renting a storage unit during the few months that your home is on the market.

CHAPTER 5 – GETTING YOUR HOME MARKET-READY

After making minor repairs, de-cluttering, re-arranging bedroom closets and kitchen cabinets, and renting a storage unit, your home should sparkle like a diamond on a bright sunny day. You should scrutinize your accomplishment with a smile, then open the front door and go outside. Does the house welcome potential buyers? Imagining how the house will look to a buyer will tell you if your home is ready to make its debut.

You will likely have many different emotions—relief, exhaustion, excitement and likely, a little sadness. Be proud at how much you've accomplished. Now, it's go time! You are finished and your home is ready to be placed on the market and presented to buyers!

About The Author

Michael Lewis

Lewis Real Estate Group
3624 Long Prairie #100
Flower Mound, TX 75022

(972) 691-7005

michael@michaellewisteam.com

www.michaellewisteam.com

Michael Lewis has been successfully selling real estate in the Dallas/Fort Worth metroplex since early 2001 and is consistently recognized by the Texas Real Estate Commission Dallas/Fort Worth metroplex as being in the top 1% of all real estate agents in Texas.

Michael Lewis brings extensive knowledge and experience to his real estate career gained from previously owning several prosperous companies. A thriving entrepreneur, Michael currently owns and operates Lewis Real Estate Group. He believes and works with a servant's mentality teaching in his local real estate community while becoming a leader in helping other agents achieve success.

Michael is a graduate of North Central Texas College. His practice is deeply rooted in educating buyers and sellers and walking with them step-by-step to ensure their success in achieving their dreams of home ownership.

6

Staging
For Top Dollar

Kimberlee Canducci
Griffin Realty Group
Plymouth, Massachusetts

Some things about buying and selling a home don't change much, even with the plethora of multimedia technology used to market a home. No matter how a buyer first learns about your home or views it online, at some point they will need to see it in person. When buyers come to view your home, you will want to show it off to its fullest potential.

Staging can increase the appeal of almost any home being offered for sale, from modest starter homes to high-end dream homes. You've probably seen the dramatic before and after photos on popular real estate TV shows. The results can be positively amazing. Staging your home does not only improve its appeal, it can also improve its value. Home staging can make a sale, turning a skeptical buyer into a homeowner.

Remember the old adage that you never get a second chance to make a first impression? It applies to homes too. Studies show that a buyer will likely form an opinion of your home within the first three minutes. That's not much time to make a great first impression but is where the art of home staging can have its biggest impact.

It's not about you.
The biggest challenge for most sellers is shifting their focus from living in their home to selling it. You must put yourself in the buyer's shoes and think about how new owners might use the space. Remember, you're selling the *home*, not your life style!

So what are some simple yet effective ways to get the most for your money from staging? First and foremost, home staging isn't as much about decorating as it is about positioning to get a buyer to say "I love this home!' People buy on emotion, on feelings of warmth and happiness, and when a home feels warm, cozy, and inviting it can subtly nudge buyers toward a decision to purchase.

Home stagers don't want to decorate your home; they want to give buyers ideas of the possibilities your home offers by creating scenes that buyers can see themselves enjoying and helping them envision how they could use the space. Rooms are re-arranged to allow easy traffic flow, furniture is grouped in small and pleasing settings, and decorations are added to provide a feeling of warmth.

To really understand what home staging is, it's helpful first to understand what it is not. Home staging is not just cleaning; it's not just clearing away the clutter, its not making all the small repairs that have piled up over the years. Maintenance tasks won't boost the price because they're expected to be done. So while all these things are important, they're actually the pre-sale tasks that get a home ready for staging.

One of first things a home stager will do is analyze the traffic patterns in the in the home. It's important to know how people move about in the house so that furniture and accessories can be arranged in ways that improve the normal flow. Furniture will be set in vignettes–small groupings that encourage people to sit and socialize. Decorations will be used to emphasize different ways the buyer might use the space, such as a tray with a tea cup and dessert plate placed on an ottoman near the TV. Décor can signal a warm welcome, such as a bowl of fresh apples and pears on the kitchen table. There will be fresh dishtowels in the kitchen, fresh boxes of tissues in easy-to-find corners, and light fixtures will have new bulbs, in a soft white rather than harsh incandescent light. The attention is in the details and all of these little touches help to make prospective buyers feel at home.

The next step in good home staging is the placement of larger decorations. Bookshelves, artwork, and knickknacks should all be arranged to draw the buyer's eyes to particular features. If you want the buyer to focus on the brick hearth and fireplace, then small, eye-catching pieces should be placed on the mantelpiece. A painting of a forest set between two windows will cause buyers to focus on that wall, on the windows, and on their particularly good view of the tall oak outside…

Most importantly, stagers will carry themes from one room to another tying everything together with color continuity, theme, and flow. These are some of the most important components of good home staging.

How much does home staging cost?
All of this sounds impressive, and in real estate, impressive sometimes can mean expensive. Professional staging rates vary from $500 to $5,000 but the good news is that staging does not always need to involve spending lots of money. Sometimes simple techniques can turn a modest home into showcase. Ultimately, how much you invest will depend on the size of your home, the number of rooms that need

staging, and the time required to prepare the rooms or the exterior of the home. Having a well-cleaned and neat home can help to keep staging costs down. The decision to stage your home shouldn't be made based on how much it will cost; but rather by how much it will increase your bottom line. The return on investment can be surprisingly high. Even small changes can make a big difference. Nationwide studies by Homegain.com and others have shown that properly staged homes sell faster and command higher sale prices, than similar homes which have not been staged.

Doing it yourself? Small, inexpensive improvements and home staging can make a big difference to your bottom line. Follow these 10 simple tips for success:

1 - Create the illusion of space
The number one goal in staging your home is to make it appear open and spacious. This applies to every room, including the garage, and even to closets and cabinets. When these areas are stuffed full, buyers automatically think the spaces are smaller than they actually are. Remove unnecessary clothing from the closets, and take a cue from closet organization companies by arranging your clothes by color to give a pleasing, organized effect.

2 - Rent a storage unit
It may not be your first choice, but consider renting a storage unit. Knowing you have a place to put things can make it easier to make decisions on what to keep in the house and what to remove. When in doubt, pack it away so buyers will

focus on the best features of the room, like an attractively designed window or a fireplace and hearth.

3 - Bring in light and fresh air

Can you smell last night's dinner? Do you have pets? Circulate fresh air throughout your home, wash all the windows, and let in as much light as possible.

4 - Define spaces

When a larger room can be used for different functions, it helps to define specific areas of use. For example, one part of a family room may be used for TV viewing; another part may have a game table set up, while a separate corner or nook can feature a comfortable chair, colorful quilt and an open book.

5 - Use the Rule of Three

Items placed together in groups of three are pleasing to the eye.

6 - Choose neutral colors

Throughout your home, colors should be neutral so buyers can envision their furniture placed in the room. Beige is the best choice, not only for walls but for carpets, too. Add splashes of color with accent pieces like pillows, artwork, and other decorative items, and place vases of fresh flowers wherever you can.

7 - Use scale to your advantage

Place artwork either at or just below eye level. Remove pieces of furniture if they make a room look cramped or small.

8 - Shine a light on it

Install bright light bulbs in fixtures and turn on all the lights when showing the home.

9 - Don't forget the garage

Is there room for the car? Hang tools on the walls and place gardening implements and supplies on shelves. If your budget allows, power wash the floor and apply a coat of paint formulated for that purpose.

10 - Add curb appeal

The very first thing a buyer sees is the outside of your home. Trim overgrown plants, pull weeds, add fresh mulch, and plant inexpensive, colorful flowers. If flowerbeds aren't an option, place a pot of flowers on the front steps. Set out a new welcome mat, replace old exterior light fixtures with an attractive lantern and install shiny new house numbers, making sure that the metals match. For example, if the lantern is made of brass, then use brass house numbers too. Put away toys, hang up the garden hose, and clean the lawn furniture.

Where to start

Focus on the kitchen, master bedroom and bathrooms. Don't make the mistake of using the kitchen as a catch-all. Remove appliances from counter tops, take magnets off the refrigerator and keep surfaces as clear as possible. Adding a bowl of lemons brings freshness and color.

The master bedroom should be an oasis of calm from the chaos of everyday life. Pay attention to small details. Use matching lampshades and have an attractively made bed with new comforter, shams and throw pillows.

Bathrooms are often small so do what you can to create the illusion of space. Use light colors on the walls, and unify the theme by coordinating the shower curtain with rugs and towels. Big fluffy white towels are especially inviting (think luxury hotel and spa). Set out a display of decorative soaps and store away everything but essential toiletries. If you have a linen closet, fold all the towels the same way so they're all the same size. Same goes for the sheets.

Getting your home ready to sell for top dollar takes some thought but doesn't have to take a lot of money. Remember that the goal is to make your home warm, cozy and inviting. Making the *right* changes is more important than making a lot of changes! Following these simple guidelines will help your home sell faster and for more money in any market.

About The Author

Kimberlee Canducci

Griffin Realty Group
385 Court Street
Plymouth, MA 02360

(508) 746-0800

kimcandu@gmail.com
kimcandu@dannygriffin.com

www.KimCandu.com

Kimberlee Canducci is a real estate broker, marketing consultant, speaker, and Internet marketing strategist who leverages the power of on-line marketing to provide her clients with instant, up-to-date information to help them buy or sell.

During her career, Kimberlee co-owned a buyer agency in Southeastern Massachusetts and was featured in Billion Dollar Agent – Lessons Learned, a collection of interviews with 70 top real estate agents who have sold over $1 billion in their career, or are on track to do so. She co-hosted the Smart Home Buying radio show and was a featured guest on Law Talk, a live call-in show about real estate. Kimberlee also produced the Smart Home Buyer Seminars series for four years.

Prior to becoming a real estate agent, she spent 18 years in marketing and sales in the microelectronics industry where she worked on projects that developed her skills in marketing communications. Kimberlee has taken her years of corporate experience in client relations and uses it to bring a professional, results-driven approach to real estate sales.

7

What to Ask Potential Agents

Amy Coleman
Golden State Realty Group
Sacramento, California

ANSWERS FROM EXPERTS ON SELLING A HOME

Take a minute to think back on your last interview. Do you have that picture in your head? Were you prepared with a clean, well-written resume, dressed appropriately, and ready to take on the world? You were determined to get that job, right? You filled out the application, sat with your potential boss, and answered questions. Did you get the job? Were you really prepared and ready? This is exactly the process you need to use when hiring a real estate agent to sell your home.

Selling your home is probably one of the most important financial decisions you will make in your life, so it should be taken seriously. Are you going to make money, lose money, or need money for repairs?

The saying, not all things are created equal, is 100% true with real estate agents. If you decide to use a real estate professional to market and sell your home, make sure to have a list of questions ready to ask the agents that you interview. This will help you find the best real estate agent for the job.

Choosing an agent is one of those big decisions that can cost or save you thousands of dollars. Some specific questions can help to ensure that you get the best representation available. Some real estate agents might prefer that you do not ask these questions, because the knowledge you will gain from their answers will disqualify them from consideration. Your questions should be designed to provide a good idea of the outcome you can expect from using their services.

Hiring a real estate professional is like any other hiring process, except you are on the boss's side of the desk. It's crucial that you make the right decision about who will handle your sale, so plan ahead. Prepare for the meeting by having a written list of questions to ask each of the agents you interview. It helps to create a 1 through10 rating system in different categories to easily and fairly compare the agents and the services they provide.

10 Questions to ask before you hire an agent:

1 - What makes you different? Why should I hire YOU?
The real estate market is ever changing. This swinging real estate pendulum moves from buyer's market to seller's market and back again. The market may be very different from when you purchased your home and technology has made it far more competitive. You will want to know the unique marketing plans and programs each agent has in place to ensure that your home stands out from other competing homes. It is important to know whether selling real estate is the agent's full-time job and how long they have been doing it. Consider the things each agent offers that others don't and whether that difference could sell your home faster and for more money. That is what you want, right?

2- What is your track record and reputation in the market?
Everywhere you look, real estate professionals are bragging about being #1 for one thing or another, quoting their statistics. Everyone can't be number one, so agents sometimes create a title for themselves. You may be interviewing the number one agent at selling yellow houses on Thursdays! A little digging can reveal the source of their statistics. If you are like many home owners, you have probably become immune

to much of this information. After all, why should you care about how many homes one agent has sold over another?

Actually, an agent's recent sales are important because it can indicate how much money they have to market your home. If the agent hasn't sold a home in months, don't you think the money they earned on their last sale has been spent to pay for their own home? The bottom line is that success in real estate means selling homes. If one agent is selling several homes every month and another is selling only a handful all year, ask why this might be. What things are they doing differently? Which do you want working for you?

3 - What are your marketing plans for my home?
Agents should not be in the business of *listing* homes; they should be in the business of *selling* them! Ask how much time and money each agent spends on marketing and compare their answer with the answers of the other agents you interview. Get specifics about which media outlets they use (Internet, newspaper, mailers, magazine, TV, etc). Do they use technology? Can they prove the effectiveness of one advertising medium over another? Ask for examples of their ads, web sites, and other marketing materials.

4 - How many homes have YOU sold in my area?
Agents should provide a detailed list of their own sales and other comparable sales in the area. This will enable you to understand how active they are in your area and also how much other homes like yours have sold for in your neighborhood.

5 - Does your Broker control your advertising or do you?

If the agent is not in control of their advertising, then your home may be competing for advertising space, not only with the agent's other listings, but also with all of the homes listed by other agents in the brokerage. Agents who sell a lot of homes typically have their own advertising budget and are not affected by the other agents in their brokerage.

6 - How close is your selling price to the asking price?

This information is available to agents on the local Multiple Listing Services (MLS), but make sure you ask this question. Is this agent's performance higher or lower than the MLS average? Their performance will help you determine whether the agent is trying to "buy" your business by promising a suspiciously high price that they cannot deliver. Do you really want to hire an agent who overpromises and under-delivers? Many sellers fall prey to this tactic because they don't want to face the truth about the true value of their home. Overpricing your home will not sell it. In fact, overpriced homes typically sell for less than if they had been priced right from the start. It is important to choose an agent who has a track record of performance, can back their price with data, and is willing to lose your business by being honest with you.

7 - On average, how long does it take your homes to sell?

This information, referred to as "Days on Market" is available from the local MLS. Do properties listed with this agent tend to sell faster or slower than the MLS average? Their performance can help you predict how long your home will be on the market before it sells. Several factors can determine how long your home will take to sell. You will want to know each agent's average time on market and their marketing plan for your home.

8 - How many Buyers do you have waiting?

Agents who attract many buyers have a better chance of selling your home. Most buyers have specific requirements for a home. Matching the amenities of your home with the agents' "Buyer in Waiting" list can sometimes produce a buyer immediately. Buyers who have been waiting for a home that fits their specific criteria will typically offer more than other buyers because they know homes that fit their criteria are a scarce commodity. This can produce an "auction-like" atmosphere where many buyers bid on your home at the same time. Multiple buyers create demand which results in higher offers for your home. Be sure to ask the real estate professional to describe the system they use to attract buyers! If their answer is, "the MLS", find another agent!

9 - Do you have past clients I could contact?

References are important, so ask to see reference notes, letters, surveys, and contact numbers from the agent's past clients. Think back to your last interview. Did your resume provide references? Ask for references of recent clients who used the agent to sell their home. Contact these people to ask if the agent communicated well during the process and whether they followed through on their promises. The most important question to ask is, "Would you use this agent again?"

10 - Can I cancel my listing agreement if I'm not happy?

CHAPTER 7 – WHAT TO ASK POTENTIAL AGENTS

Be wary of real estate agents who want to lock you into a lengthy listing contract. Agents can get out of these contracts by ceasing to effectively market your home but you can't. Within the listing agreement, there are usually penalties and protection periods to safeguard the agent's interests, but not yours. How confident is the agent in the services they provide? Will they allow you to cancel the contract without a penalty if you are not satisfied with their service? Do they have a written cancellation guarantee?

These ten questions should help you find the best agent to market and sell your home. After each interview, take time to evaluate each agent's responses carefully and objectively. Use the rating system you created before the interview to rank the agent on how well they answered each of the questions. Who will do the best job for you? These questions should help you decide which candidate is best qualified to sell your home!

About The Author

Amy Coleman

Golden State Realty Group
3835 N Freeway Blvd. Suite 140
Sacramento, CA 95834

(916) 960-1774

amy@colemanhammer.com

www.sacramentohousefinder.com

Amy Coleman was born and raised in Sacramento and attended Sacramento's top notch Business Marketing Program at California State University. While in college, she consulted, marketed and managed cosmetics for a nationwide chain. Amy has a passion for people and a natural ability to listen to their needs, explain their options, and convert them to friends. In 1999, Amy found an opportunity in real estate that utilized her marketing degree, her outgoing personality, and allowed her to help others achieve their dream of home ownership. Amy continues to educate herself to provide her clients and friends with innovative choices that best fit their needs. Amy also owns a property management firm to assist clients in managing wealth-building investment properties.

Amy ranks in the top 1% of all agents in Sacramento's tri-county area. She gives back to the community by supporting the Make-A-Wish Foundation, Boys and Girls Club of America, and other children's charities. She co-founded REO4Kids to help children's chairities and co-owns Golden State Real Estate with her business partner, Bruce Hammer.

8

The Team-Selling Difference

Lynn Horner Baker
Horner Baker Partners
Marietta, Georgia

ANSWERS FROM EXPERTS ON SELLING A HOME

"Seldom do people buy logically. They buy emotionally and then justify their decisions with logic. Find ways to get them emotionally involved with your product or service." - Author unknown

The anticipated outcome of a successful home sale is generally defined as "receiving the highest possible price, in the shortest possible period of time, with the least amount of inconvenience." The practice of hiring a professional real estate agent to accomplish these goals is only the beginning of attaining the desired outcome. In any market, the art of selling a home is a combined effort of both the real estate professional and the homeowner. The parties are not mutually exclusive in achieving the best possible result. Neither the agent nor the homeowner can easily accomplish the desired outcome without the full cooperation, involvement and team effort of the other. The agent's task is to educate and advise, while the home owner's responsibility is to implement the suggestions in order to attain the maximum results of the sale.

When home owners make the initial decision to sell their home, the first step is to select several professional real estate agents to interview. Whether the preliminary selections are made based on visibility and success in the area, or a recommendation from a friend or family member, you should understand that this meeting is a two-way interview. You are looking for the agent who will sell your home fastest and for the highest price and the agent is looking for a seller who is realistic and truly motivated to sell. Both parties are qualifying the other party based on whether they will be a winning team together.

Be sure to ask the agents you interview about your part in the sales effort. If the agent does not explain the inherent relevance of your role in creating the stage for the buyer to make a decision, you might be interviewing the wrong agent!

When the interviews are complete and the best agent is hired, the real estate professional should initiate a plan of action to attract the right buyer to your home. This plan could include anywhere from twenty-five to seventy-five action items, which should have been clearly articulated during their interview presentation. The majority of these activities involve creating exposure for your home and specific marketing to identify potential buyers.

Your agent should use multiple venues for attracting the right buyer, a person who happens to be looking for a home like yours at the same time you are selling. Besides buyers, the second goal of any marketing system is to attract other agents. Your agent serves as a consultant and team leader whose expertise, knowledge and brilliant creativity facilitates a sale. The homeowner calls the plays, makes the decisions and is responsible for staging the home to create an atmosphere for buying. Details of how to do this should be clearly defined by your real estate agent.

The importance of teamwork cannot be overstated because the perception of real estate in the past twenty years is not the reality of real estate today. Supply and demand have reversed in many areas, causing an oversupply of homes. In some markets, there is only one buyer for every twenty to twenty-five homes for sale. How do you position yourself in the number one or number two slots to receive an offer on your home when the market is saturated with distressed sales at rock-bottom prices?

It becomes the responsibility of the seller to distinguish their home from other homes on the market once their agent has successfully attracted buyers to their property. Selling a home is both a price war and a beauty contest. The property that draws a buyer emotionally and holds them through the subconscious rationalization that takes place in their mind definitely has the advantage. Buyers must be able to positively experience all five senses in order to become attached to your home.

There are several factors to consider in the buyer's rationalization process with price being the first and foremost consideration. A good listing agent will educate you about the market you are competing in by providing information about other comparable properties for sale in order to establish the fair market value for your home. In any market, value is a moving target. It's simultaneously elusive and exclusive which is why it is so important to hire a professional who recognizes the value a property has to specifically targeted buyers. For instance, a two story home in a good school district may be attractive to a family with children but not to empty nesters who don't wish to climb stairs.

Pricing a home is not a precise endeavor. Sellers, buyers, and agents can use exactly the same facts to reach three entirely different opinions of fair market value. An experienced agent offers more objectivity and can provide a substantiated price range. Overpriced homes receive few if any showings and no offers because there are other available properties priced at or below market. The price that is recommended and agreed upon based on a complete evaluation of competing and sold properties should be aggressive from the first day on the market. Overpricing your home due to the old school belief that buyers will write a low offer is pure fiction. First, buyers may never view your overpriced home and, second, they may not wish to negotiate with an unrealistic and uneducated seller. Making future price reductions may be futile.

A successful home sale is a value-added transaction. Sellers and their real estate agent need to become creative in their approach and craft a unique sales offer that is not available from any other seller. This could be a monetary bonus, a service bonus, pre-paid HOA fees, a vacation, tickets to a sporting event, or some other incentive. Sometimes, a listing agent may offer to either buy the home of a potential buyer or sell it without charging a brokerage fee. This can remove a tremendous burden from the prospective buyer, enabling them to sell their existing home and purchase a new one without the stress of owning two homes. There are several real estate professionals around the county who offer this unique selling service.

Once a unique marketing system has been launched and your home is priced competitively, you must embark upon setting the stage for the buyers. Unlike any other value proposition, the goal is to under-promise and over-deliver. When the sign is placed in the front yard, the starting whistle has blown. First impressions can rarely be changed. There is a mere fifteen seconds to win or lose buyers during their initial response to your home. While first time buyers might be willing to trade a little sweat equity for a lower price, move-up buyers have already experienced that and this time their expectation is that everything should be perfect.

Staging a home works well to add emotional value for which a buyer is willing to pay. The ultimate goal of the home owner is to create a visual presentation of a lifestyle and the potential that lifestyle provides to the new homeowner. The paradigm shift is recognizing that the selling point of a home is the *lifestyle* it provides to the new buyer, not the features or amenities of the home.

Buyers purchase the homes that they can mentally and psychologically move into. This is why it is imperative that personal effects and photos be packed away. Clutter should not just be minimized, but removed entirely from sight. Something seemingly innocuous, such as packed and stacked boxes in the garage, could be a red flag to a buyer who sees those boxes as a sign that the home does not have sufficient storage. Cleanliness is paramount as is a well-maintained, well-cared-for, well-lighted home. Investing in fresh paint, including the trim, can return double or triple its cost. Professional landscaping can have the same beneficial effects.

Create a ritual of hospitality in a comfortable environment in which the potential buyer can relax and absorb the energy of the home. This doubles the charm and appeal they experience. In appealing to all five senses, soft classical music is an inviting backdrop and alluring aromas can easily be concocted with a few drops of vanilla extract in a shallow pan of water in a warm oven. A plate of cookies and cold bottled water is also a practical approach to keeping buyers in your home longer, envisioning how they will entertain their own family and guests. The lighting should be bright, including lights in every room, bathroom, closet and definitely the terrace. Blinds and shades should be open to let natural sunlight flow through the home, another positive force on the psyche of the buyer.

Team-selling is the close, coordinated effort of a professional real estate agent and a well-educated, motivated and cooperative homeowner. Both should be committed to the premise of selling for the highest dollar value, in a reasonable time without headaches, surprises or a breakdown in expectations. A great real estate agent will provide the professional knowledge, outline the exact process, manage expectations and be an educated and pro-active team leader. The motivated seller is the support player who is coachable and willing to put in the effort to realize their goals. There is a right way and a wrong way to sell a home and the final result unequivocally produces dramatically different results. Every seller looking for the highest price and best terms would be wise to hire an experienced listing agent who doubles as a great team leader.

About The Author

Lynn Horner Baker

Horner Baker Partners
111 Village Pkwy, Bldg 2, Ste 201
Marietta, GA 30067

(770) 579-4060

sold@lynnhornerbaker.com

www.hornerbakerpartners.com

Lynn Horner Baker has sold homes in Atlanta, GA since 1991 and has been recognized with multiple awards beginning with "Rookie of the Year" and continuing to being named the number 4 Individual RE/MAX Agent in the state of Georgia and Top 10 Board of Real Estate Agents for the past 18 years. Having sold thousands of homes, Lynn's primary objective is always to provide excellent service, unparalleled knowledge, and a personal commitment to achieving the financial goals of her clients. Lynn is the owner and President of two real estate brokerages and her son, Chase Horner, is the Qualifying Broker of both companies. Together they lead a top-producing team which supports their commitment to excellence.

Lynn coaches real estate professionals throughout North America for the Craig Proctor Real Estate Coaching program. Voted "Woman of the Year" 2010 by the National Association of Professional Women, Lynn is involved in the local chapter of NAPW as well as the East Cobb Business Association and the Golden Retriever Rescue Association. Lynn can often be seen on tennis courts or jogging along the Chattahoochee River.

9

Does the MLS Really Work?

Aaron Kinn

Kinn Real Estate
Keller, Texas

Many home sellers often ask the question, "Does marketing really help to sell my home?" The answer is yes, marketing really does play a huge role in whether a home will sell. The first thing to understand is that there is a huge difference between marketing and *effective* marketing. This chapter will lay out an effective marketing plan using the Multiple Listing Service (MLS) to help sell a home, and why it is so important to choose the right agent who will position your home to receive the most attention on the MLS.

Many home sellers believe that the MLS is just a tool for real estate agents to find their home and show it to their buyers. While this may have been true in the past, now anybody with an Internet connection can log on and view the properties on the MLS. Most real estate agents across the country use the MLS as their primary tool to market a seller's home. Most MLS systems are exclusive, allowing only real estate agent members to market homes on their site. For buyers, it's a different story. The MLS is syndicated across the Internet, allowing buyers from all over the world to view any property at any time from the comfort of their home.

The syndication of MLS listings is the biggest reason that your listing needs to be perfect. Huge national and international listing services draw millions of buyers to their sites each month. The information they distribute is an exact copy of the information real estate agents use to market homes locally for their sellers. The photos, descriptions, and other details about your home (including misspellings) are available for the world-wide public to see. This is why the MLS has turned into one of the most important marketing tools used in selling homes.

Many agents and nationally-known websites use Internet Data Exchange (IDX). Realtor.com was one of the first IDX websites, but now there are literally hundreds of companies creating personalized IDX solutions for real estate agents. This allows tech-savvy agents to advertise every MLS listing as their own as long as there is some sort of credit given to the agent who actually listed the property. This means that sellers who use a tech-savvy agent could have hundreds of agents advertising their property to literally thousands of buyers across the country and all over the world!

The most important thing to understand about the MLS and IDX syndication is that only the seller-hired listing agent can make updates, changes or additions to the original MLS listing. Even when other agents see a mistake, a poor description, or the lack of a photo, they cannot make changes to the listing. Thus, it is extremely important how the initial listing for your property appears on the MLS.

This critical information is what separates average real estate agents from great real estate marketers. When looking at listings on these public sites it becomes very obvious that many real estate agents don't take the time and care necessary to properly market a home on the MLS. Many real estate agents upload only a front photo with a non-compelling description, and minimal information about the property.

It is often difficult to find accurate room sizes, school information, or detailed information about amenities in the home that most buyers are looking for. Shockingly, nearly one out of ten property listings do not include any photos at all! How would prospective buyers become interested in your home if you can't show off its best features? When there are no photos, most buyers assume the worst and skip over your home, never inquiring about or going to see it. The MLS can be either your best asset or the biggest hindrance to selling your home.

Photos are one of the most important aspects of the MLS. The right photos can intrigue buyers and leave them wanting more. When you pique their interest, they usually want to look inside your home. An unflattering or unattractive picture can turn buyers away, even if the home is perfect for them. Most buyers click through the MLS on the Internet, with each home appearing with a photo and a brief description. In the blink of an eye, they make the decision on whether to click to the next home or click on yours to get more information. The photo is the key to capturing or quelling the interest of a potential home buyer.

What constitutes a bad photo in the MLS? As an example, your home may have white cabinets, but there may be a recent trend that buyers no longer desire white cabinets. Your kitchen may also have granite countertops, which is a very desirable attribute to buyers. If a photo is taken of the entire kitchen with the white cabinets visible, buyers may pass up your home because of the cabinets. The solution then, is to take a photo from the kitchen looking across the granite countertops and into the living room. The photo prominently displays the countertops, but leaves the cabinets out of view. Seemingly minor marketing details like this can be the difference between selling and not selling your home.

Another common mistake made by many real estate agents is only using one photo of the property. In this digital age, everything is available at the click of a button. Most MLS services can accommodate dozens of photos and a lengthy description of each. There is no reason not to have multiple photos of your property. If the MLS listing for your property doesn't offer multiple photos, it will not receive the attention it deserves. In fact, the search function in many online MLS systems allows buyers to filter out the listings that do not feature multiple photos!

In some cases, sellers should consider hiring a professional photographer to capture the look and feel of their home. The photos in the MLS are the single biggest attractor of potential buyers to your property so this should be taken seriously. If the initial photo attracts a potential buyer, they will view the description. Like the photos, the description can make or break a potential buyer's interest. Truly, the skills of a wordsmith are needed in this situation. Often, one word or letter or the lack of that word or letter can make a huge difference on how your home is portrayed on the MLS. Take a look at the following example:

"Beautiful Mountain view from living room of this stunning home"

"Beautiful Mountain views from living room of this stunning home"

The only difference in the second description is the addition of one little "s," to pluralize the feature of mountain views, but that simple addition adds a great deal of power to the MLS description for this particular property. Below is another example:

"Gorgeous home located on the golf course. Great floor plan with kitchen opening into the living room"

"Stunning executive home located on the third fairway of Champions Golf Course. Inviting floor plan features spacious kitchen with granite counter tops, gas range, and a center island which opens to living room with cozy wood burning fireplace and spectacular views from floor to ceiling windows."

The first description was taken verbatim from the local MLS. The second description is a reworked version of the very same home! Which do you think would appeal more to potential buyers? The second version took more creative thought and a little more work, but likely would make a huge difference in selling this home. Another huge mistake agents make is including the bedroom and bathroom count in the property description. The phrase below is one that can be found in any MLS system across the country:

"This beautiful 3 bedroom, 2 bath home has two large living areas…"

Unfortunately, the description above is taking away precious space from the marketing of the property. Most MLS systems limit the number of characters allowed to describe a property. Being clear and concise while describing the home's benefits—not the features—is very important. Giving the bedroom and bathroom count only restates the obvious. Every IDX and MLS website already states the number of bedrooms and bathrooms in the home and often provides the number of living areas, garage stalls, square footage and year built. Often, these vague descriptions provide no real value to the buyer or the home owner trying to sell their home.

Describing other amenities, such as room sizes, school district, and energy-saving "green" features are more vital in selling a home. When it comes to describing amenities and pertinent details, more is better. The points made here apply to all types of advertising, both on-line and in print. That is why MLS advertising is not only a useful tool in marketing a home, but is actually the most crucial tool in the marketing strategy.

Agents may use many other marketing methods, but none carry the same importance as the MLS listing. Ineffective or uninspiring marketing remarks in the MLS can be the sole reason a home doesn't sell, not necessarily its price or condition. Marketing is and always will be the most important part of selling a home!

About The Author

Aaron Kinn

Kinn Real Estate
1668 Keller Parkway, Suite 400
Keller, TX 76248

(817) 380-5610

aaron@aaronkinn.com

www.aaronkinn.com

Aaron Kinn is a Texas real estate broker, licensed for more than a decade. Aaron and his business partners sell real estate in Dallas, Tarrant, Denton, Johnson, Ellis, Hood, Parker, and Wise counties in Texas. Over the past ten years, Aaron has helped over 1,000 people achieve the American dream.

Born in Rochelle, Illinois, Aaron attended Monmouth College where he obtained a Bachelor of Arts degree in 1998. After graduating college, Aaron became a High School Art teacher. He coached baseball and basketball for four years until he discovered his passion for real estate.

After starting his real estate career as the Rookie of the Year, Aaron became a top producer among the 50 agents at his company. He is ranked in the top 1% of agents in the Dallas/Fort Worth area and believes in giving back to the community. He belongs to REO4Kids, a national group whose members give to children's charities for every home sold. Aaron's biggest passion is being the best dad that he can be to his daughter, Eva!

10

Market-Based Pricing

Bob Zachmeier
Win3 Realty
Tucson, Arizona

ANSWERS FROM EXPERTS ON SELLING A HOME

The most common question asked in real estate is typically, "How is the market?" My answer is always the same, "it depends..." In order to properly answer the question I need to know whether the person asking is a buyer or a seller, what it is that they anticipate buying or selling, the price range at which they will be competing, and the area where the property is located.

The media often describes a real estate market as either a "Buyer's Market" or "Seller's Market" but there are several sub-market variables which define supply and demand on a much smaller scale. Sub-markets can be distinguished from the overall market by isolating homes based on property type, price range, and area. These variables can make a specific market vastly different than the overall market, so it is important to find an expert who understands your specific market and has a track record of consistent performance in it.

In a free market economy, the "market value" of any commodity is the price a buyer is willing to pay and a seller is willing to accept. In an "arm's length" transaction where the buyer and seller are unrelated and there are no other incentives other than the commodity being exchanged, price is determined by the supply and demand at the time of the sale.

When there are more buyers than sellers, prices typically increase due to buyers offering a higher price to gain a competitive advantage over other buyers. This condition is referred to as a "Seller's Market" because demand is greater than the supply and sellers enjoy the luxury of having multiple buyers compete for their property.

CHAPTER 10 – MARKET-BASED PRICING

Conversely, a "Buyer's Market" develops when more properties are for sale than there are buyers to purchase them. Prices typically decrease in over-supplied markets as the most desperate sellers compete with one another in price-lowering contests to attract buyers.

Before setting a price for your home or even advertising it for sale, it is important to understand the market in which you'll be competing. The best source of this information is a real estate agent who actively tracks the market. Agents who sell only a few homes all year will not have their "thumb on the pulse" of the market like the agents who sell homes every week. Without current market information it is difficult to know what is attracting buyers or how quickly your property type, price range, and area are selling.

Property Type

In 2012, prices in Tucson, AZ bottomed and interest rates were at historic lows. Single-family homes priced around $100,000 were selling as fast as we could list them but condos and town homes listed at *half* the price were difficult to sell. Why? The association fees of many town homes and condos were as much or more than the mortgage payment! This in effect, doubled the cost of owning the property. Why would a buyer choose to live in a condo or town home when they could have a home with more space, a garage, and a private yard for the same monthly payment?

Figure 6-1 shows the percentage of available homes sold in February, 2012 by property type. Those who were selling single-family homes enjoyed a 22% success rate, but only 12%

of condo owners were successful. Owners of mobile homes during this time had only a 5% success rate, which is a 95% failure rate! Do you think this information would be important to know before pricing your property?

Figure 6-1 Sales by Property Type

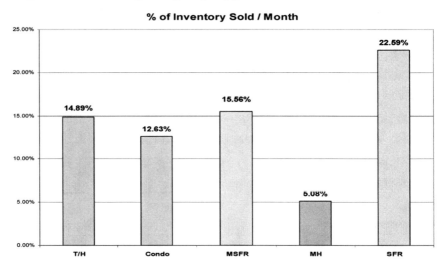

% of Inventory Sold / Month

Price Range

Market supply and demand can vary greatly at different price ranges. The balance or imbalance is another important thing to consider before deciding on a list price for your home. For example, in February, 2012 nearly 50% of the homes priced between $100,000 and $120,000 were sold but only 2.5% of the homes priced over $1,000,000 were sold. It's safe to say that few if any home sellers would not be satisfied with a 97.5% failure rate! With so few buyers at this price range, these homes were actually the best "deals" on the market, but when buyers are uncertain about the economy, they downsize instead of taking on the risk of a higher mortgage payment.

Figure 6-2 Sales by Property Type

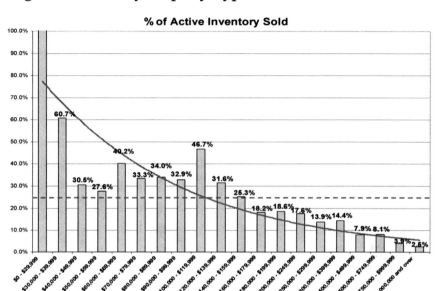

If your home is close to a major price break, it may make sense to price it a few thousand dollars below market value. As illustrated in Figure 6-2, a home valued at $122,000 would have a 31.6% chance of selling but at $119,500 the odds are increased to 46.7%. When nearly half of the available homes are being absorbed by the market each month, the most desirable homes often create bidding wars which can drive offers much higher than the asking price. Check the demand at various price points before setting your asking price! It could make your home the site of a bidding war instead of a ghost town.

Area

Prices can vary by tens of thousands of dollars in a matter of a few feet when homes are located on the edge of a subdivision or near a school district boundary line. These man-made boundaries can literally put your next door neighbor's home in a different market area. If an adjacent subdivision is a gated community, homes could sell 10 to 15% higher, even if they have the same floor plan! School districts can also make a big difference, especially when test scores are significantly higher or lower in an adjacent school district.

Homes in outlying areas are typically much less expensive than properties in close proximity to jobs, schools, and social activities. The lower prices are offset by longer drive times and higher fuel expenses. When gasoline prices increase, the demand for outlying properties is significantly diminished and this can severely impact home prices in the area.

Another factor buyers consider is the orientation of your lot, especially in areas that have mountain, water, or city light views. Homes that offer the desired views from the living areas and back yard are often sold at higher prices than homes that don't offer the view. In areas like Arizona with intense summer heat, East-facing back yards sell at a premium because they are shaded and enjoyable in the afternoon while homes across the street are baking in direct sunlight late into the evening.

How is the market? Now you can agree *it depends!* Before selling, you need to determine the supply and demand for each property type, price range and area by charting the percentage of available homes being sold each month in each subtype. You also need to size up your competition.

Sizing Up Your Competition

Very few people begin their home search by choosing a certain street on which to live. Unless buyers are relocating next door to a close friend or a disabled relative, most will embark on a much wider search based on where they work, where they worship, or where they would like their children to attend school.

For this reason, you should conduct a radius search to find all of the homes for sale, under contract, and sold within a two-mile radius of your home. This will establish the overall supply and demand in your area. By filtering the data by year built, square footage, subdivision, and lot orientation where applicable, you can compare your home to others with similar amenities that are currently listed or have recently sold.

Overpricing
Unfortunately, many sellers choose the real estate agent who promises them the highest sale price. Don't fall for this trick! It leads to an overpriced home that sits on the market unsold. The only showings will be from agents who use your overpriced home to get their clients to write an offer on another home. Don't be the *bait* that helps another home sell!

Unscrupulous agents use this tactic to get your listing but you can easily catch them in the act! When interviewing prospective real estate agents, require that they provide the MLS history of the last five homes they've sold. This sheet will show how recently the agent's sales occurred, the number of times the sellers had to reduce their price in order to sell, and the length of time it took to sell each property they listed.

Don't be fooled by a report showing the sale price compared to the list price. You need to see how closely the homes sold to the agent's *original* list price, not the *last* list price. The MLS history sheets are a good indicator of how well the agent understands the market and performs on their promises. Don't kill the messenger! Hire the agent who is honest about your home's value, not one who promises what they can't deliver and then profits from your loss.

After twelve years and thousands of home sales, I've never had a client go from house to house asking, "How much do the sellers owe on this one?" Buyers don't care how much you owe or how much you spent improving your property. They decide on whether to visit your home by how well it compares to the other homes they've found in their search. Thanks to the Internet, today's buyers are highly educated. If your price is too high, they will *never* view your home and you won't sell it if you can't get buyers inside to see it.

Even if you lower your price later (the intent of the high-bidding agent all along) buyers may still stay away. Homes that have been on the market a long time give buyers the impression that something is wrong with them. You only get one chance to make a first impression and the initial price is the first impression your home makes on the market.

Your initial list price has a lot to do with how fast and for how much your home will sell. Before deciding on a price for your home, hire a competent agent and assume the role of the buyer by checking out the competition. By comparing your home to others like it, you'll be able to see your home from a buyer's point of view. This can help you get past the emotional attachment you have after years of living in your home.

About The Author

Bob Zachmeier

Win3 Realty
2474 E River Road
Tucson, AZ 85718

(520) 690-WIN3

bob@win3realty.com

www.win3realty.com

Bob Zachmeier was born and raised in Mandan, ND. His parents showed by example that determination and a strong work ethic could achieve almost any goal.

As the third of six children, Bob learned early in life to become self-reliant. At the age of sixteen, he owned a fireworks business, complete with billboard and radio advertising. The business helped to fund his college education and that of several siblings.

He became a part-time real estate agent in 2000 at the age of forty and by 2002 was earning enough from real estate investments to leave his job as a manufacturing engineer after twenty-two-years at Texas Instruments and later Raytheon's Defense Electronics division in Tucson, Arizona.

In 2004, Bob and his wife, Camille, founded Win3 Realty. The name reflects their desire to create a win-win-win situation for their clients, the community, and the agents, staff, and owners of their company.

Four years after starting Win3 Realty, their team was number one among 6,000 agents in overall sales and buyer-side transactions. With only twelve agents on their team, they've continually pushed the bar higher; selling more than 2,000 homes in the tough Arizona market between 2008 and 2011.

Zachmeier shares his success with others by speaking at national conferences and by holding real estate training seminars for agents across North America. His events have produced over $100,000 for children's charities like the Make-A-Wish Foundation and Boys and Girls Clubs of America. He co-founded REO4Kids, an elite national group of real estate agents who give proceeds from every sale to children's charities and received the "Spirit of Philanthropy" award from the National Association of Fundraising Professionals.

By sharing his experience and practical advice as a real estate broker, coach, college instructor, author, lecturer, and philanthropist, Bob Zachmeier has helped thousands of people improve their financial well-being.

Zachmeier has written and published three other books; *Upside Up Real Estate Investing* – a "how to" book on real estate investing, *SOLD On Change!* – a step-by-step description of how he grew his real estate business by 1,000% in three years, and *A Daily Difference* – how ordinary people can integrate charitable giving into their daily lives.

To find these and additional titles visit the publisher's website at www.outoftheboxbooks.com or contact the author via e-mail at: bob@bobzachmeier.com.

11

Pricing For Maximum Value

Warren Flax

Platinum Realty Team
**Yardley, Pennsylvania /
Windsor, New Jersey**

ANSWERS FROM EXPERTS ON SELLING A HOME

The mailman is wrong! Homes are never "going" for a certain price. Homeowners who want to sell their home often say they have been told that similar homes in the neighborhood are "going" for x-amount of money. This often means that the mailman, or some other uninformed person, told the homeowner about a house that had an asking price of x-amount three years ago. Because the people moved out and new people moved in, they assume that the home was sold for the asking price.

Other homes have likely been sold in the neighborhood more recently for higher or lower prices, but people believe what they want to believe. A lower price won't stick in a seller's mind as well as the higher price quoted by the mailman. Often the home the mailman is referring to did start out at the high asking price, but the price was lowered several times before finally being sold. In some cases, the home didn't sell so the owners rented it out. This happens a lot. The point is that there are tried and true methods of pricing a home to sell every time in every market. They have nothing to do with burying little statues in your yard or taking advice from someone in a totally unrelated profession.

Wise sellers think like *buyers*. How would a buyer narrow down the myriad of choices they have? In most major metropolitan areas there are thousands of homes for sale at any time. Buyers start out with a wide variety of options and begin narrowing their search from there. The four most common criteria that buyers use to narrow the field are: location, property type, size, and condition.

CHAPTER 11 – PRICING FOR MAXIMUM VALUE

When selling, there are five simple steps that will help you net the maximum return from your home:

1.) Define the market

2.) Use current market data to determine how many of the available homes are selling each month

3.) Narrow choices by using the same parameters that buyers use to search for homes

4.) View recently sold, pending, and active homes similar to your home to establish a price range

5.) Factor in the amenities of your home to determine the price at which it is most likely to sell.

Step 1: Define the market

A market can be defined by the school district, zip code, or a specific neighborhood or subdivision. A real estate broker who is an expert in that market will know how buyers define the market when they search for a home. Every home for sale within this market is your competition—not just the houses in close proximity of your home. In terms of distance, the comparisons will depend on the nature of your home's surroundings.

Usually, when your home is appraised, it is compared to others within a half mile in a city, within one mile in a suburb, and within five miles in a rural area. This is how an appraiser thinks, but many families search by school district. This means that you are competing with all of the other homes in the school district offering the same number of bedrooms and bathrooms, even the homes "way across town." If the property is in the same school district, it could mean that it is in direct competition with your home.

Step 2: Use market data

The best way to determine the strength of your market is to calculate the *absorption rate*. The absorption rate is simply the percentage of available homes being sold each month. If 10% of all the listed homes are selling, there is a 10 month supply of homes available, but if 50% of the listed homes are selling, there is only a 2 month supply of homes on the market.

This information can help sellers determine how aggressively to price their home in order to compete with other homes for sale. When the search is filtered to include only the homes like yours, the absorption rate will clearly demonstrate how many buyers are looking for your type of home, in your area, at this snapshot in time. When pricing a home, there is not a more important question to ask.

To calculate the absorption rate in your area, you must first determine how many homes are currently for sale in the defined market area. The next step is to determine how many homes in the market area have been sold in the past 30 days. If there are 77 homes currently for sale and 7 were sold in the past 30 days, then it will take 11 months to absorb the current inventory. Put another way, there are 11 homes available for each qualified and motivated buyer. This means that your home has a 9% chance of being sold if priced the same as the other competing homes.

Step 3: Narrow choices by refining search parameters

The number of bedrooms (or square footage in urban areas) is the most common parameter buyers use to search for homes. If a family needs four bedrooms, then the homes they will consider are limited to those with four bedrooms or more. As mentioned previously, buyers also narrow their search by price, property type (single family detached, twin, townhome, condo etc), number of bathrooms, and lot size.

Step 4: Analyze the status of other homes on the market

By reviewing the homes like yours that have sold in the past three months, homes currently under contract (pending), and homes actively listed for sale, you can determine the likely price range at which your home should sell. In an appreciating market, homes that are active and pending will be priced higher than homes than have recently sold. However, in a declining market, active sales must be priced lower than homes that sold a few months prior. This is necessary because a home sold two months ago would have gone under contract about four months earlier, and the market has declined since then. In appreciating markets, actively listed homes are often listed considerably higher than homes recently sold.

Step 5: Determine the likely price range of your home

How do your home's condition and features fit into the range of choices available to buyers? Sellers should seek the opinion of an objective outsider to compare the condition and features of their home to other homes currently for sale. To give sellers insight on how buyers will compare their home, many top-selling brokers take their seller clients in person to see four or five competing homes that are similar to theirs.

At this point, should you spend money on a home that you are planning to sell? Although each situation is different, the general consensus is that in order to net the highest possible amount, you should do everything possible to clean and de-clutter your home so it will show at its very best. This can include minor repairs such as touch-up paint, carpet cleaning, drywall repair and basic exterior landscaping.

The time for major home improvements such as upgrading a dated kitchen or bathroom has passed. Sellers lose money on most major improvements unless they are contractors and can do the job themselves, incurring only the wholesale cost of materials. National statistics routinely show that major improvements cost more than they generate in additional sale price.

A typical Comparable Market Analyses (CMA) consists of three or four recent sales that are similar in size and location to your home. An appraisal consists of three recent sales and three actively listed homes. Both CMAs and appraisals can fall short in accurately predicting the value of your home. Just because there are three similar homes within a mile which were sold for $300,000, $310,000 and $320,000 within the past six months doesn't mean that your home will sell between $300,000 and $320,000.

Based only on those three sales, it might make sense to price your home at $309,900 or $319,900 but in the real world, buyers have more choices than just the three examples of past sales used in the appraisal. If there are 19 homes currently for sale in the same market area for less than 300,000, and all have the same number of bedrooms and bathrooms as your home, why would a buyer even schedule a showing to see yours if it is priced at $319,900? This is how most pricing mistakes are made.

A few sales may "support" the academic parameters used to appraise homes, but do not provide the same view of the market from a buyer's standpoint. The appraisal is critical once a buyer chooses a home, negotiates a contract, and applies for a loan, but it doesn't help to get a buyer inside to look at your home!

The title of this chapter is "Pricing for Maximum Value" not "Pricing a Home to Rot on the Market for a Year and Attract Only Lowball Offers from Greedy Investors." These five easy steps should help you get the maximum amount possible for your home so you can sell it and move on with your life. As an informed seller, you can now tell your mailman to stick to what he does best… delivering the mail!

About The Author
Warren Flax
Platinum Realty Team
301 Oxford Valley Rd, Suite 201A
Yardley, PA 19067
and
92 N Main St. #18E
Windsor, NJ 08561-0414
(215) 945-3000
warren@prtemail.com
www.warrenflax.com

Warren Flax was born and raised in Philadelphia, PA, and graduated from Carnegie Mellon University. He earned a Masters degree from Wharton School and the Lauder Institute at the University of Pennsylvania. In 1991 he volunteered in Israel during the first Persian Gulf War and survived 39 Scud missile attacks while working at a hospital base near Tel Aviv.

Upon returning home, Warren began anchoring and reporting television sports at stations in Bakersfield, CA, Ft. Myers, FL, and Seattle, WA. In 1998 he returned to Israel to volunteer while studying Hebrew and working on an agricultural kibbutz. He also worked in Tel Aviv translating and editing documents, including for then-defense Minister and eventual Prime Minister Ariel Sharon.

Warren moved to South America to study Spanish and work in his family's art material business. While there, he met and married his wife, Rocio. After the arrival of their children, Julia and Joshua, Warren became a real estate agent in 2003. He currently has offices in Pennsylvania and New Jersey.

12

Setting the Right Price

Joey Trombley
Kavanaugh Realty
Rouses Point, New York

ANSWERS FROM EXPERTS ON SELLING A HOME

When it comes to selling your home, setting the right price is one of the most important decisions you will have to make. If you set the price too high, no one will come to see your home. Without getting buyers inside to even look at your home, you will not be able to sell it. Buyers will purchase other homes in the area offering similar amenities at a cheaper price because they represent a better value.

You don't want to under-price your home either. Setting your price too low can result in a sale at far lower than your home's actual value, costing you thousands of dollars. So how do you establish the right price for your home? There are a few ways that you can do this:

Option A - You can look at local home guides and public records to see what other properties are selling for.

Option B - You can have an independent appraiser do an evaluation for you

Option C - You can have a real estate agent conduct a fair market evaluation for you.

Using the home guides referenced in Option A is not a good way of establishing the value of your home because you are comparing your home to the prices that other homes are *listed* for instead of how much they are actually selling for. The ads are at least a few weeks old by the time the magazines are printed and many of the homes are overpriced. By following this pricing strategy, your home will be just another overpriced home on the market.

CHAPTER 12 – SETTING THE RIGHT PRICE

Hiring an appraiser, as recommended in Option B is a good option because the appraiser has no emotional ties to your home. Appraisers are licensed with the state and have to follow a strict set of guidelines. You will receive a neutral and honest assessment of what your home is worth based on what other homes have sold for in the area. The downside is that it will cost you hundreds of dollars to have this done.

Option C - Having a real estate agent provide an opinion of value is also a good option because the real estate agent will search for similar home sales just like an appraiser would but will also take into account the supply and demand of the market. The downside is that you have to be leery of agents who try to "buy" the listing on your home by offering to sell it at an unrealistically high price.

These unscrupulous agents will tell you what you what you want to hear so they can put their sign in your yard. They know your home won't sell for the price they've promised and rely on the assumption that you will lower your price several times over the term of their listing agreement. The other reason these agents are willing to set an unrealistic price for your home is to get calls from interested buyers. Although the buyers will not be interested in your overpriced home, the agent will sell them another home which is fairly priced. Beware of agents who quote a suspiciously high value for your home. If it sounds too good to be true, it probably is!

Imagine spending the time to clean and prepare your home for a showing to prospective buyers. Your hope is that they will like your home enough to make an offer, but in reality the agent may only be showing your home to illustrate to their buyers how reasonably another home is priced.

Don't put yourself in this position! Buyers make offers on the homes that represent the best value. Your home is only worth as much as a buyer is willing to pay, so it is vital that you have established the fair market value for your home before you put it on the market. It is important to understand the real estate market so you can calculate whether the value of your home matches the reason you are selling.

When interviewing real estate agents, be sure to ask whether they can provide a "net sheet" for you that will itemize all of your closing costs, the amount you need to pay off your mortgage, and any other fees you may owe. The net sheet will provide a realistic picture of how much of the proceeds you will walk away with after the sale. When you know the amount you can expect to keep, you have to ask yourself whether the amount will enable you to achieve the goals you set before deciding to sell.

Whether your goal is to downsize and move closer to your grandchildren or upsize in preparation for another child, the market value of your home is whatever other similar homes are selling for in your area at the time. It doesn't matter that you want or need a certain amount to pay off your mortgage, your credit card, or your car. Unfortunately, buyers don't care that you are moving to another area where homes are more expensive. This is why it is vital to get the market value right the first time.

CHAPTER 12 – SETTING THE RIGHT PRICE

By choosing a reasonable price and going over the net sheet before listing your home, you will have a realistic idea of what you can expect from the sale of your home. The market won't give some sellers what they are hoping for because they do not have realistic expectations. If that is the case, the market may be telling you to hang on to your home until prices increase. Unfortunately, the seller's needs have no bearing on the value a buyer places on your home. Find an honest agent to help you determine whether selling is the right choice for you.

About The Author

Joey Trombley

Kavanaugh Realty
36 Champlain St
Rouses Point, NY 12979

(518) 572-0441

joey@joeytrombley.com

www.joeytrombley.com

Joey Trombley has been in the real estate business for 27 years. He's been the Broker/Owner of Kavanaugh Realty, nestled in upstate NY for the past 19 years.

Joey has been involved in Craig Proctor's Quantum Leap coaching for 13 years and has been coaching real estate agents in the program for the past 5 years. The Kavanaugh Realty team consistently outsells all other teams in the area and Joey's personal sales consistently rank in the top three individuals on the Real Estate Board.

Joey has been married for 26 years and has three children. Gaelan went to Plattsburgh State and currently works on the real estate team. Sagan is attending the State University in Albany, NY, and Maura is in high school.

13

Focusing On Net Proceeds

Chase Horner
Horner Baker Partners
Marietta, Georgia

Home owners who to attempt to sell their home without the aid of a real estate agent are often referred to as a "For Sale By Owner" or "FSBO" (pronounced *fizz-bow*). Statistics confirm that the prime motivation of FSBO sellers is the perception that they will save money by eliminating part or all of the real estate commission. Another reason for going FSBO could be the seller's pride telling them that they can do a better job of selling their home by going it alone.

Either way, this uninformed economic decision is often made because sellers don't clearly understand what real estate brokers actually do to sell homes. In the profile of Home Buyers and Sellers released in 2011 by the National Association of Realtors' (NAR), 37% of FSBO sellers simply did not want to pay a commission. This boils down to money, pure and simple.

While cost-saving success stories are not all fairy tales, the vast majority of FSBO sellers would have "netted" more proceeds in less time if they had utilized the experience and knowledge of a real estate professional. NAR estimates that 23% of all FSBO sellers fail to price their home correctly, which ultimately results in lower net proceeds. The study found that FSBO transactions account for only 10% of all sales and interestingly, when private sales to friends, relatives, or other acquaintances are factored in, the percentage of successful FSBO sales drops to just 6% of the open market. By attracting only one buyer at a time FSBO sellers effectively eliminate any competition for their home, negating the "auction effect" that real estate brokers can generate with proven selling systems and vast market exposure. Their money-saving strategy does them a huge disservice, putting less in their pocket.

CHAPTER 13 – FOCUSING ON NET PROCEEDS

Selling a home is a full-time job, especially if you don't already have selling systems in place. Before attempting to sell on your own, ask yourself how much time, energy and resources you are willing to commit to selling your home. The process is detailed and demanding, especially in highly competitive, oversupplied markets. Sophisticated tools and sales techniques are required to compete in the information age. If you are considering selling your home on your own, these important questions should be answered:

How much money can be allocated toward marketing?

Who will create marketing fliers?

Do fliers really work or are they merely for nosy neighbors?

What type of signage will you use?

Will you use 1-800 numbers with call capture technology?

How much time can you allocate for open houses?

How will you orchestrate an online marketing strategy?

How will you compel real estate agents to show your home when the common perception is that they will not be compensated?

What is the best way to convert online leads into showing appointments and, ultimately, offers?

How will you handle buyers interested in touring your home?

Who will expertly guide the contract negotiation process?

Who will manage the appraisal and negotiate the inspections?

Above all, who will vigilantly shepherd the executed agreement through the selling process to closing?

Clearly, there are a lot of questions that demand answers. An experienced real estate broker can easily out-gun a FSBO seller through greater exposure and leverage in the Multiple Listing Service (MLS), the only place many agents search for homes for their clients.

A good real estate broker utilizes an extensive marketing system which includes direct marketing, on line pay-per-click campaigns, and sophisticated Internet search engine optimization (SEO) to showcase your home. They administer a labyrinth of syndicated websites, unleash tools to capture leads, manage a team of licensed agents to convert the leads into viable buyers, and employ a full time staff to manage the myriad details of each transaction. Simply put, real estate brokers have a much broader net to cast with hundreds of professional connections, sophisticated business systems, and powerful tools that a FSBO seller simply cannot match. If you can honestly match these qualifications, then go for it, but it is unlikely that you can.

If you still decide to sell on your own, proceed with caution. Going FSBO could not only be an expensive decision, but possibly a litigious one. One of the more critical components to consider is legal exposure. Chances are that a licensed real estate broker representing a buyer will ultimately sell your property. The FSBO, at this point, is negotiating with a professional agent and ultimately paying the agent to negotiate against them. Everything favors the buyer in this case. A FSBO seller is not usually educated in contract law and is not aware of the consequences of all the terms and conditions of the contract. Knowledge of time limits, special stipulations, inclusion or exclusion of certain exhibits, and the requirements of different types of loans, are just a few areas where inexperience can be costly. Hiring a qualified real estate broker to represent you not only ensures adherence to legal requirements, but also guarantees that all aspects of the transaction are subject to a strict Code of Ethics.

Figure 17-1 – The Decline of FSBO Transactions

The chart in Figure 17-1 shows the steady, decade-long decline in the percentage of FSBO transactions. In 2011, only 10% of all transactions (down from 19% in 1991) were FSBO sales. Are the shrinking numbers due to the poor success rate in an oversupplied, highly competitive market, or simply due to the increasing time, money, technical competency, and expertise required to facilitate a sale? Whatever the case may be, more sellers are opting to place the task of selling their home in a professional's hands.

About The Author

Chase Horner

Horner Baker Partners
111 Village Pkwy, Bldg 2, Ste 201
Marietta, GA 30067

(770) 579-4060

chase@hornerbakerpartners.com

www.hornerbakerpartners.com

Passion, energy and focus—these are the tenets with which Chase Horner runs his business. As the Principal Broker of both Horner Baker Partners Real Estate and Horner Baker Partners Metro in Atlanta, GA, Chase diligently oversees all aspects of each brokerage.

He is a long-time member of the Craig Proctor Real Estate Coaching Program—one of the nation's most successful networks of brokers, an active member of the *National REO Brokers Association*, and an active Board Member of the International Association of Real Estate Experts. Over the course of his career, Chase has directed hundreds of successful real estate transactions. An alumnus of Emory University, Chase lives in Atlanta with his wife Dena and his Frisbee dog, Marshall.

14

The Real Cost of Selling

Dawn McCurdy
McCurdy Real Estate Group
Latham, New York

The term "closing costs" has many different interpretations. For the sake of this chapter, closing costs will be considered any expense associated with the preparation and selling of a home. There are both fixed and variable expenses. Fixed costs are flat fees directly related to the sale of a home, including the fees paid to the professionals involved in the transaction. Variable costs include a myriad of items that can vary in amount based on the work involved or purchase price of the home.

Many people are surprised at all the costs associated with selling a property. It is important for sellers to be aware in advance so unexpected fees don't pop up at the closing table. The following items are all considered "normal" costs of selling and must be included in calculations so you'll have a reasonably close expectation of how much you will net on the sale of your home:

- Real estate agent's commission
- Holding costs
- Home preparation (repairs, fix-ups and staging)
- Tax, title and legal fees
- Moving expenses

Real Estate Agent's Commission

Some homeowners believe that they can save money by not using an agent for representation and instead try selling their home as a For Sale by Owner, also known as "FSBO." Sometimes, they are able to save some money, but typically there will be a much larger cost in terms of time, worry, and

CHAPTER 14 – THE REAL COST OF SELLING

hassle. All of these factors can have a financial impact that may not have been considered during initial "savings" calculations.

Often, the first question potential sellers ask a real estate agent is, "how much is your commission?" When asked why that is their primary concern, they typically respond, "we want to know how much it's going to cost us to sell our home. The real estate agent is our biggest expense and we want to minimize the cost as much as possible."

Real estate agent commissions vary by area and can be a flat fee, a percentage of the sale price, or both, but it's most common for agents to charge a percentage of the sale price on a residential sale. The amount of commission and the services provided vary greatly between agents. Not all agents are created equal so find out what services are provided before trying to negotiate the commission.

There are many services an agent performs, but what differentiates good agents from great agents is the education they provide to the seller. A great agent will explain all of the costs involved in selling a home and will provide the seller with a "net sheet" which lists all of the expenses anticipated at the time the home is listed and again when an offer is received.

Upon executing a listing agreement with an agent, a seller should be sure that the agent's commission is clearly stated in the contract as well as a description of the services included in the fee.

111

Whether selling your home on your own or with the help of an agent, there are costs associated with marketing your home. Sellers who enlist the services of a real estate agent pay a commission but save themselves the hassle of learning as they go by trying to sell their home on their own.

Many sellers who start out trying to sell on their own home are unsuccessful and end up hiring a real estate agent. This can be costly because you must pay your own marketing expenses in addition to paying an agent. A knowledgeable real estate agent will increase the exposure your home receives. Often times, attracting more qualified buyers in a shorter period of time will increase your net proceeds, offsetting much or all of the real estate agent's fee.

In addition to an agent's commission, sellers will incur expenses before, during, and after the sale that can make a huge financial impact on their bottom line. An experienced agent can minimize these expenses by negotiating the best terms for you throughout the transaction.

Holding Costs

Holding costs are obligations paid every month that your home is unsold. These costs include mortgage payments, utility bills, property taxes, hazard insurance, HOA fees, maintenance, and repairs. An agent who exposes your home to a vast market of interested buyers typically creates a quicker sale which can save thousands of dollars in holding costs. The combined costs can exceed one percent of your home's value every month your home is not sold!

Copies of your property taxes and HOA fees should be provided to your agent, the Title Company, or attorney for proration at the time of closing. It is important to keep current on your bills and know the amount needed for each expense in order to calculate the amount you will keep after the sale of your home.

Preparing Your Home

Home Inspection: The cost of a home inspection can vary widely depending on the age and size of your home and how well it has been maintained. Prior to listing your home, it makes sense to get a home inspection to identify problems that could become an issue later. Plan on paying between $250 and $500 for a home inspection, though the cost could be more or less depending on the size of your home and the area in which you live. A pre-listing home inspection can save a lot of money, time, and aggravation in the future.

Home Warranty: A home warranty can be a great benefit to the current homeowner and their future buyer. For a nominal cost (about $300 to $500, paid at closing) sellers can buy a warranty on their home that will cover unexpected repairs while their home is on the market. After closing, the policy will cover buyers for up to thirteen months after the sale. A home warranty can make your home more favorable than competing homes being considered, especially by first-time home buyers with limited funds and experience to make repairs. It can lead to a faster sale and a higher offer price because buyers have the comfort of knowing that they will be covered if something unexpected occurs.

Repairs: Repairs and/or upgrades should be considered to prepare your home for the market. Some items may be more costly than others, so you'll want to invest in improvements which yield the highest return on the eventual sale, both in terms of the sale price and the time on market. Some updates may include:

- Carpeting/Flooring
- Landscape/Exterior maintenance
- Painting (inside and out)
- Remodeling (minor)
- Appliances

No matter how new your home is, repairs may be required by the buyer's lender or requested by the buyer as a condition of purchasing your home. These repairs can be very minimal or extensive. An experienced agent can guide you through the customary items required by many lenders.

Staging: Home staging can often help to achieve a faster sale and a higher price. Some sellers may choose to employ the services of a professional staging consultant. This cost can be as low as $100 for a consultation fee to several thousand dollars for complete staging. The cost depends on the size of your home and the degree of staging you choose. Sellers should defer to their staging consultant for advice while keeping in mind that this service can result in a higher sale price and decreased market time.

Buyers' Closing Costs: It has become almost customary that sellers contribute to the buyers' closing costs in order to get their home sold. Sellers who agree to a closing cost allowance should be sure to deduct that amount from the sale price of the home when calculating their net proceeds. Closing costs can range from two to six percent of the purchase price, so sellers should discuss the costs with their agent or lawyer before accepting an offer.

Legal Costs

Whether attorneys or title companies are used to facilitate a sale varies from state to state. Fees range from a flat fee to an hourly rate schedule. The clock starts ticking upon review of the contract, so sellers should be sure to ask about this fee before beginning the transaction.

Property Taxes: No matter when a home is sold, the seller is responsible for the taxes pertaining to the property up to the day of title transfer. Check the laws in your area. If you have pre-paid the property taxes for the year, you may be entitled to a credit instead of a bill at closing. There may also be other refunds on pre-paid escrow accounts and hazard insurance. If there are outstanding taxes that you overlooked or were unable to pay prior to closing, the title company will take the funds directly from the proceeds at the closing to satisfy the outstanding amounts to enable a clean transfer of title.

Transfer Fees: Real estate transfer fees are state and local taxes that are assessed when real property is transferred between parties. The amount varies from state to state but the fee is usually calculated on the actual sale price of your home.

An experienced real estate agent will be able to provide an estimate of your potential liability in their net sheet.

Mortgage Payoff: Any existing mortgages or liens on your property must be paid and satisfied prior to the transfer of title or the sale of your home. Ask your lender for a prorated payoff statement through the day of closing, including any pre-payment penalties and fees charged for servicing the loan.

Moving Costs

The costs of moving your belongings from one home to another should be considered when calculating the cost of selling your home. You may pay as little as $1,000 for a cross-town move or as much as $12,000 for a cross-country move. It is a good idea to get two estimates from insured, reputable movers before putting your home on the market. Moving costs can vary greatly depending on how many belongings you have and whether packing and storage are included. A mover should provide a written estimate that outlines the time, weight, number of boxes, and personnel required to complete your move.

Other Costs

There are a few miscellaneous costs associated with moving from one home to another that are not directly related to the sale itself. These expenses may include school transfer fees, gym fees, storage locker fees, and others.

All fees on the settlement statement will be explained to you at the closing table by the escrow officer or attorney. If you find anything that wasn't expected, be sure to bring it to the escrow officer, attorney, and agent's attention. Some fees can be waived, so be sure to bring them up!

Even without adding all of the miscellaneous costs, it is easy to see how the costs associated with selling your home can significantly reduce the amount of your proceeds. Fortunately, some of the costs are deductible on your income taxes. Conferring with a qualified accountant and financial advisor is always recommended, as they are familiar with the ever-changing tax and government guidelines.

About The Author

Dawn McCurdy

McCurdy Real Estate Group
1004 New Loudon Rd, PO Box 456
Latham, NY 12110

(518) 785-9900 - Office
(518) 441-3538 - Mobile

dmccurdy@mccurdyrealestate.com

www.mccurdyrealestate.com

Dawn McCurdy was born and raised in Albany, NY and has been selling real estate in the Capital Region since 1985. She is Broker/Owner of The McCurdy Real Estate Group, Inc. and has helped more than 3,000 families. Her business is founded on trust from past clients, who refer their friends and family.

McCurdy leads a team of like-minded colleagues who she coaches to continually bring their businesses to the next level. She is a mentor to her agents as well as many in the industry. Dawn's commitment to her clients and her team is to overcome everyday challenges using her strengths, skills, talents, energy and enthusiasm to their advantage.

Dawn holds many real estate designations, a Paralegal degree, and belongs to numerous local organizations. Being a director of her local Chamber, she is very involved in her community and contributes to multiple charities on a local and national level. Dawn resides in Colonie, NY with her husband, Phil, and twin daughters, Amber & Taylor.

15

Changing the Outcome

Igor Krasnoperov
Rising Star Realty
Mohegan Lake, New York

ANSWERS FROM EXPERTS ON SELLING A HOME

Selling a home is a process that sellers should be prepared for, sometimes months in advance. You should think of it as a challenge, with the end goal of successfully selling your home for the most money and in the shortest period of time. There are a limited number of home buyers at any given time. Without careful planning, other home sellers might be celebrating the victory instead of you. A few things that are often overlooked by sellers can potentially cost thousands of dollars, in addition to lost time and a lot of frustration.

Property Taxes

Most buyers searching for a home will have a pretty good idea how much they can afford to spend each month. The monthly payment on their mortgage typically includes principle, interest, property taxes, and insurance. Many sellers believe that property taxes are what they are, and if buyers like their home enough they will buy it. While that might be true, the question is *at what price?*

Property taxes can account for a large portion of your buyer's monthly payment and if there is a big difference in the amount of property tax on similarly priced homes, buyers will definitely notice. Homes with higher property taxes than similar homes in the area are more difficult to sell and often sell for less money. Tax laws and rates vary from one area to another, but if you live in an area with high property taxes, pay special attention to the assessment you are being taxed on.

Imagine that your property taxes are $1,200 per year higher than a competing home for sale down the street. A buyer will have to pay $100 more every month if they buy your home. Depending upon the interest rate of their loan, $100 per month could service the debt on $15,000 to $20,000. Buyers will always choose nicer amenities over higher property taxes if the payment is the same!

In addition, most buyers expect that their property taxes will go even higher over time. What can a home owner do to change the outcome of this situation? While you can adjust your price to compensate for the high taxes, you could potentially do better by challenging the tax and getting it reduced.

Municipalities have different rules regarding the re-assessment of properties, but it is important to know that property taxes are based on a home's assessed value. It is up to the homeowner to challenge the assessed value if it is incorrect. Unless you bring it to the tax assessor's attention, your home's valuation and taxes will very likely remain unchanged.

You may find that your home's value is higher than its assessed value—which means you are not paying as much as you should in property taxes, but if you find that the value of your home is lower than the assessed value, immediate action should be taken. Contact the tax assessor to ask for tax grievance paperwork and try to arrange an informal meeting. The assistance of a real estate agent, who is knowledgeable about area values, tax assessments, and the grievance process, is recommended.

Because the grievance review is typically done only once a year during a specific period of time, you need to initiate this process well before putting your home on the market. You can have an informal meeting with the tax assessor at any time and may be able to resolve the grievance right then and there. If not, you will have to wait for "grievance day," the specific day of the year designated by the local government to review assessment complaints. Once again, the assistance of a knowledgeable real estate agent is strongly recommended, as the result of these meetings can affect the future marketability of your home.

Protecting Privacy While Marketing Your Home

Many sellers overlook the need to protect their privacy while they have their home on the market. When the topic of privacy comes up, many people think of personal documents, but the need for privacy extends beyond that. Don't leave your bills on the kitchen table, assuming that potential buyers will not touch your personal mail. Why take the chance? Any important paperwork, especially any which is related to your financial situation, should be put away out of sight as it could adversely affect the amount of a buyer's offer on your home.

Sellers who have religious decorations in their home should probably put them away. While there is nothing wrong with displays of this type, you never know what a buyer's personal beliefs and prejudices might be. It is best to be cautious and attempt to maintain a neutral presentation of your home.

Finally, you need to be careful about the answering machine attached to your home phone. Make sure that the volume is turned down or muted entirely. The last thing you want is for a potential buyer to overhear a phone message about your financial situation or other offers on your home.

Home Improvements That Don't Pay

Homes that don't require repairs or improvements will sell faster and for more money than those that do, but not all home improvements pay off. This can vary from one area to another, and also depends on the price range of the property.

In most cases, home owners make improvements based on their own preferences, and don't necessarily take the resale return of those improvements into consideration. Most people would love to have an updated bathroom, a custom kitchen with high-end appliances, beautiful landscaping, and other amenities. While buyers might love the $75,000 custom kitchen, they probably won't be willing to pay that much for it.

So, what major improvements should a home owner consider doing first? According to Remodeling Magazine, no remodeling projects will produce a 100% return on the money invested in them, but certain projects yield a better return than others. For example, a major repair such as a roof replacement usually returns only 60% of its cost, but an improvement such as this is worth making as it would be difficult to sell a home with a leaky roof. While the returns vary from one region to another, improvements to siding, windows, kitchens, and baths seem to be consistent top performers.

Most buyers look for a home that has no deferred maintenance, newer appliances, and updated plumbing, electrical, and heating systems. Many buyers wish to simply move in, unpack, and move on with their lives. Anything that you can do to make your home "move-in ready" will provide an advantage over competing sellers. Your home will sell faster and for more money if you make the transition easy for potential buyers. Nobody likes to deal with hassles.

Great Photos Attract Buyers

Do sellers really need the services of a professional photographer or can they just snap a few exterior photos with a point-and-shoot camera to get their home sold? Really, the question is a no-brainer. Good photos attract the attention of more buyers. When buyers go online to browse for homes on the market, many of the photos they see will be of low quality. The importance of a good first impression cannot be overstated, and in this case, the photos that potential buyers see create their first impression of your home. Don't "roll the dice" with your first impression. Make sure that the photos on display are of the best quality.

While photography is more of an art than a science, the photographer must understand what they are trying to accomplish with their photos. Your goal is not to show every corner of your home, but rather to capture your home's selling features in the best possible light. A great photo can paint an amazing story in the potential buyer's imagination. The process of buying a home is very emotional and great photos can trigger very strong and very positive emotions in potential buyers.

Make sure that the first four photos of the home are the most attractive pictures available. This is important because first impressions are important, but also because many marketing portals use only four photos. You'll need to consider what impression these photos will have on potential buyers. If the photos only show the exterior of your home, buyers may assume that something is wrong with the home's interior. Consider the best features of your home, perhaps a vaulted ceiling or a stone fireplace, and make sure to capture those amenities in the marketing photos. Your goal is to "wow" potential buyers from the beginning to give them a reason to want to come inside your home.

Virtual tours have been around for a long time, and vary from a basic slide slows with still images to interactive 360-degree panoramas. In my experience, the properties that feature virtual tours receive more online attention than those that don't.

Selling a home, especially in today's market is a fiercely competitive process. It is often the "little things" that can change your outcome, so if you want to be successful do your utmost to be educated about the process and take note of the little things that will make a difference.

About The Author

Igor Krasnoperov

Rising Star Realty
1750 East Main St
Mohegan Lake, NY 10547

(914) 243-4885

igor@mysellingsystem.com

www.mysellingsystem.com

Igor Krasnoperov has worked in real estate in the Hudson Valley region of New York since 2001. From 2003 to 2010, Igor was an Associate Broker with Re/Max Classic Realty, where he was recognized with the Re/Max Network's "Hall of Fame" award. In 2009, Igor was named Top RE/MAX Agent in the Hudson Valley region, and the number two agent in New York State, in number of transactions and gross commission income. Igor has also received numerous Diamond Awards (the highest level of recognition) from the local Board.

In 2010, Igor opened Rising Star Realty & Property Management, Inc, his own brokerage. Igor and his team recognize that their clients are their best marketing source. Continuing education is a very important part of Igor's business philosophy. He has been a member of The Craig Proctor Real Estate Coaching Program since 2003, and has attended numerous conferences and courses to stay on top of the ever-changing real estate laws, marketing approaches, and technology trends.

16

If Your Home Doesn't Sell

Willie Miranda

Miranda Real Estate

Clifton Park, New York

ANSWERS FROM EXPERTS ON SELLING A HOME

Trying to sell your home can be a daunting task. For those who have had their home on the market for several months with little or no activity, the notion of it actually selling may seem like a pipe dream. If this is the case, you likely need to reformulate your strategy. There are many things that can be done to sell a home and every home will sell with the proper tools in place.

The most common reason that your home will not sell is that the price is too high. If your home has been on the market for a while, you may need a substantial price reduction. One of the best barometers in determining whether your home is priced too high is the number of showings each month. If your home is getting only a handful of showings, it is likely that prospective buyers are finding other homes that offer more value at a lower price.

As a seller, it is important to look at your home through the eyes of a buyer. If there are other homes like yours for sale in the neighborhood, you will need to price your home so that it stands apart from other competing homes. If there are a limited number of buyers for a particular area, sellers need to do whatever they can to avoid pricing themselves out of the market. Markets are local, so your agent should have firsthand experience in knowing what home buyers value most in the area.

It is very important to be truthful and objective with your price. If other homes for sale are similar in size and style, it is important to find out what differentiates your home from the competition. Perhaps your home has an updated kitchen

128

and bathroom, while the competition has a finished basement. Lot size, garage space, number of bedrooms and bathrooms all can add or subtract value when comparing one home to another. A good real estate agent will take these things into consideration when determining fair market value of your home.

You need to realize that every buyer who comes through your home is likely to have seen other homes in the area that are also for sale. After looking at all available homes, buyers will decide which home represents the best value. If you are selling your home, you are in direct competition with other homeowners who also are selling.

Price is the first thing that buyers think about. If buyers feel that a home is priced too high they will not make an offer, even if they like the home. Since the real estate market is dynamic and ever-changing, it may be worthwhile to have an appraisal done. This is perhaps the best way to determine what the asking price should be. Buyers looking to purchase a home are likely to need a mortgage and thus will need to hire an appraiser anyway.

It is important to be aware of the market in your local community. Sellers have the upper hand in markets where there are a low number of houses for sale. This results in a limited selection of homes from which buyers have to choose. When there are many homes for sale, buyers have the advantage because sellers are forced to compete against one another. While there are national trends in the housing market, specific areas can differ tremendously due to supply and demand for certain types of homes.

In either a buyer's market or a seller's market if your home is not selling, changes need to be made to your marketing and advertising strategy. Your real estate agent should be able to provide specific details about the best methods being utilized to sell homes in your area. Just as technology has changed the way people go about their day-to-day activities, it has also changed the way that most buyers approach the home buying process.

Each day, more and more people utilize the Internet to search for homes. There are thousands of websites that allow buyers to gather information on homes for sale. It is vital that your agent's marketing plan includes Internet advertising. While print ads may still serve a purpose, successful marketing plans focus on capturing buyers who are viewing homes online.

Another important piece of a marketing plan is signage. There are many interesting ways that prospective buyers can obtain information about the homes they drive by. Some agents still provide paper sheets attached to their sign for interested buyers but there are technological advancements that have made things much easier and less wasteful. For example, if buyers do not wish to speak with an agent trying to sell them a home, they now have the option to have the property information texted directly to their cellular phone. Smartphone users can scan a QR (quick response) barcode that immediately links them to a webpage designed specifically for the property they are visiting. In our society, utilizing technology is vital to marketing a property. It is very important that your real estate agent use these techniques to ensure that your home is exposed to the maximum number of buyers.

An equally important thing to consider if your home has been sitting on the market is its cleanliness. Buyers should never walk into a cluttered home with questionable odors. Homes that are priced right and marketed well will not sell if buyers are turned off by the interior condition. Luckily, this is the easiest problem to correct. When you receive notice of a showing, make sure that your home is as tidy and as clutter-free as possible. While it is important that your home looks "lived in," buyers may be turned away by kitchen countertops cluttered with dishes and appliances, and living rooms with pet odors and carpet stains. It is important to make your home as presentable as possible. Sellers with a vacant home may need to hire someone to stage the house appropriately.

Professional staging often makes sense for both vacant and furnished properties. Those who live in their home while it is offered for sale can benefit greatly from proper staging. Often, it can be as simple as removing or repositioning existing furniture but with vacant houses, key pieces of furniture may need to be brought in. While buyers usually have an idea of where they would place their tables, couches, televisions etc., having those pieces in the right locations make it easier for buyers to imagine themselves living in the home. This can go a long way toward coaxing a buyer into making an offer.

Rather than making expensive updates, focus on the inexpensive things that can be done to make your home more attractive to buyers. Painting, de-cluttering and cleaning are the easiest. Most buyers will modify or update bathrooms, kitchens & bedrooms to fit their style, so it is not necessary to spend a lot of money in these areas. Just because you spend $10,000 updating your kitchen, doesn't necessarily mean that you are going to get all or even half of the money back when your home sells. It will certainly make your home more attractive to buyers, but it will not return as much as it cost. As long as everything is in proper working order, expensive updates do not usually need to be made. Some updates, however, are much more likely to pay off in the long run. For example, homeowners will usually get their money back on granite countertops because they hold their value over time.

If your home is not selling, the last thing you should do is panic. As discussed earlier, there are many things that can be done to help a home sell. It is important to be as realistic as possible with the price. Don't let your emotions get involved when determining the fair market value. While houses become homes because we raise our families in them, have weekend barbeques and plant gardens, these sentimental values don't translate into tangible monetary value.

Be honest with yourself about your home and take note of the issues that need work. Address the obvious issues and advertise the most appealing aspects of your home. Be forthcoming with your real estate agent by helping them formulate a plan of how together you can sell your home fast, and for top dollar.

About The Author

Willie Miranda

Miranda Real Estate Group
1482 Route 9
Clifton Park, NY 12065

(518) 348-2060

wmiranda@mrgteam.com

www.williemiranda.com

Willie Miranda started his real estate career in 1999. After winning awards at two national real estate franchises, Willie started Miranda Real Estate Group, Inc. in July, 2002, and developed a customer-service oriented team approach and an aggressive marketing plan.

Willie doesn't just hire anyone; he looks for people who share his core value of giving the customer A+ service. He manages 65 agents and 8 staff members in Clifton Park and Rotterdam, NY offices. Miranda Real Estate ranked in the top 10 in total production volume out of 480 brokers in the Capital Region of New York in 2008, 2009, and 2010. Miranda Real Estate received Business Review's "Great Places to Work Award" in 2005, 2006, 2008, 2009, 2010, and 2011.

In 2005, Willie was selected from 25,000 agents across the United States and Canada to receive Craig Proctor's coveted Quantum Leap Award, for having the most exceptional gains in real estate success. In 2006, he received the Business Review's "Forty under 40 Award."

ANSWERS FROM EXPERTS ON SELLING A HOME

Willie is known as the "Local Area Real Estate Expert," and is frequently featured on local radio shows and local area television news broadcasts, providing up-to-date information for buyers and sellers on the conditions of the current real estate market. He has had his own radio show, Capital Region Real Estate Today, and has branded himself well in the area.

His commitment to providing outstanding service to his clients and agents goes beyond the realm of just "getting the job done." He genuinely cares about his clients and the professional and personal success of every person in his organization. He is friendly and enjoys meeting people and building new relationships. He understands the importance of not only building new relationships, but nurturing them.

Willie has successfully coached over 250 real estate agents and lenders across the country on how to start-up, grow, and bring their businesses to the next level, and he continues to be seen as a leader and mentor by many in the industry.

In addition to Willie's real estate business, he owns and operates the award winning Allstate Insurance Agency, also located in Clifton Park. He has owned this company for approximately eighteen years.

Willie's wife Shari has supported him in the growth of both companies for the past eighteen years. They have two daughters, Christine and Julia, with whom he is active in softball and soccer leagues. Willie and his family reside in Clifton Park, NY.

17

Preparing For Inspections

Paul Rushforth

Paul Rushforth Real Estate
Ottawa, Ontario

ANSWERS FROM EXPERTS ON SELLING A HOME

The home-selling process can sometimes be exhausting and stressful. Interviewing agents, signing paperwork, staging, taking photos, keeping your home buyer ready, leaving during showings, and enduring nail-biting negotiations can make the process seem never ending.

When an offer is accepted and the end is almost in sight, sellers are often subjected to a home inspection where a qualified inspector goes through your home with a fine-toothed comb. This can be nerve racking, especially if you have an older home. According to the National Association of Home Inspectors, about 85 percent of home buyers conduct a home inspection. Inspections are an important part of selling your home. This chapter will help you to prepare your home for the inspection and provide tips and hints to help put your mind at ease.

First and foremost, sellers must make sure their home is spotless. This shouldn't be overlooked, as it is a reflection of how well your home has been maintained. To prepare your home for buyers, wash the floors, scrub the bathrooms, get rid of any dust throughout the house, repair leaky faucets, re-caulk around the sinks and tubs, have the chimney cleaned, replace burned out light bulbs, install new batteries in the smoke detectors and repair any broken windows.

Be mindful of the cleanliness of the furnace room as well, especially since the home inspector will be reporting on the condition of the furnace and electrical box. In addition, keep the outside of the house tidy; clean the windows, clear out the gutters, remove debris from the yard, seal cracks in the driveway, and replace any broken or damaged shingles. In the winter months, shovel the driveway and any pathways for easy mobility. It is important that the home inspector is unobstructed during the inspection, so keeping your home tidy and well-maintained is beneficial to both parties. Overall, a first impression is a lasting impression. A clean home will start the home inspection off on the right track.

The inspector will need access to all areas of the property to provide a thorough report. This includes access to the garage, attic, and any other buildings on the property such as sheds and outbuildings. Remember to leave any keys for buildings or rooms that are regularly locked to ensure the process goes as smoothly as possible. It would be a waste of time for everyone if the inspection had to be rescheduled because of such an oversight. It could even delay closing.

For vacant homes, it is important to keep the utilities activated. The inspector will need to check many aspects of the home, such as testing the appliances, furnace and electrical box. If the utilities have been disconnected, this portion of the inspection will not be possible and the inspector will have to reschedule, costing extra time and money. Again, never let an oversight such as this hold up the sale.

Many homeowners have done major renovations, as well as maintenance and minor work on their homes. Some of these jobs require permits, and sometimes warranties are provided along with documentation pertaining to the work that was done. Sellers should have all permits, warranties and invoices ready for the home inspector to review during the inspection. This information will help to answer the buyer's questions regarding work that was done previously.

One of the most common problems found during the home inspection is improper drainage or grading. This can cause leaks and moisture in a home's basement that could scare potential buyers away. Re-grading the soil around the home creates a gradual slope so water will flow away from the house. Re-grading can be more difficult on a flat lot, so you may want to consult a professional.

Faulty wiring is also something that could scare away potential buyers. Often times, homeowners will perform amateur electrical work, which can lead to inadequate overload protection, open junction boxes or mismatched wiring. This is not only dangerous, but can be quite scary for prospective buyers. Ensure that your electrical system is within code requirements before the home inspection. If you are not experienced in electrical work, hire a certified electrician to make the necessary repairs.

Next on the list of inspection issues is a damaged roof. Damaged shingles, leaks, and broken or missing flashings are a big turn-off for buyers. A new roof can be a huge expense so most homeowners avoid homes with roof issues. Some buyers actually search only for homes with a new roof because of the peace of mind that comes with it. Ensure that faulty shingles are replaced and flashings repaired where necessary. This will not only spruce up the exterior of your home, but also help to pass the home inspection.

A red flag for home inspectors, and many potential buyers, are water stains on the ceiling. This indicates the presence of a past leak that may or may not have been repaired. If the leak has been fixed, take the extra steps to treat the stain. Start by dabbing the stain with bleach. After the area dries, roll over it with a multipurpose sealer. Next, the entire ceiling will need to be painted to ensure the color is matched properly. If the leak has not been fixed, or the source of the problem has not been found, have the problem resolved before covering up the stains. This will save time and avoid future problems.

Heating, ventilation and air conditioning (HVAC) is a very important component of a home. These systems are used daily to keep your home comfortable, whether heating in the winter months or cooling in the summer months. Home owners often forget that these systems are quietly working away. Prior to listing your home, have your HVAC system checked to be sure that all components are working properly. During the inspection, the inspector will test the furnace, check the ventilation and examine the air conditioning unit. To pass the inspection, ensure that regular maintenance and repairs have been completed.

Other things that can be discovered during the home inspection include structural problems, issues with the plumbing, faulty gutters, and poor overall maintenance. Routine maintenance over many years can greatly improve your home's chance of passing the home inspection. If you have concerns about any of these items, deal with them before the home inspection.

A very important aspect of the home selling and inspection process is disclosure. You must make buyers aware of any problems that have occurred in your home such as fire or flood damage, and any repairs you have completed or hired someone else to do. It is important to be honest and up-front about damages or repairs to ensure that you are protected in the event that something happens after closing. You should discuss disclosure with your real estate agent to better understand the information that needs to be provided to the buyers during the inspection period.

The home inspection generally takes several hours. You should leave the home during this time and allow the buyer, their agent, and the home inspector full access to your property. In most cases, it is advisable that you are not home during the inspection. This allows the inspector to get the report finished without interruptions. The buyer will feel more comfortable without you being present, as they may be asking the inspector questions about the condition of your property.

Although you know much about the history of your home, an inspector is a qualified professional and an unbiased third party who can tell buyers much more. Many sellers who are present at the inspection volunteer unnecessarily to repair items that the home inspector finds. For these reasons, you should leave the home during this appointment.

Don't be concerned about the home inspection unless there is a major problem. Although the home inspector's report will address everything they find throughout your home, buyers and their agents will know that no home is perfect. The home inspector will make recommendations about repairs that need to be made and will identify areas that should be brought up to current building codes.

Some buyers may look past minor repairs that come along with the home and some may factor this into their negotiations. Contract adjustments could come in the form of a lower offer price or an additional clause requiring that the seller make the necessary repairs prior to closing. In some instances, the buyer may walk away from the home because of repairs that concern them.

Ask your agent questions regarding disclosure, the home inspection, or any other issues that might arise. Inspections are an important part of the real estate transaction but proper preparation can save you time, money, and even the sale. Failing to prepare in advance could undermine your negotiating power against buyers who have done their homework.

About The Author

Paul Rushforth

Paul Rushforth Real Estate
3002 St. Joseph Blvd
Ottawa, Ontario K1E 1E2

(613) 788-2122

information@paulrushforth.com

www.paulrushforth.com

Following a 10-year professional hockey career in North America and Europe as both a player and assistant coach, Paul decided to bring his enthusiasm, dedication and organizational skills to real estate. In 2004, Paul traded his hockey jersey for a suit and tie and has since built a real estate empire that is nothing short of Stanley Cup material. Since 2007, the Paul Rushforth Team has ranked as the #1 Residential Real Estate Team in Ottawa and finished 2009 as #1 Keller Williams Team Worldwide. Early in 2011, Paul opened his own real estate company, Paul Rushforth Real Estate, Inc. with no end in sight.

Building a reputable & successful real estate team has allowed Paul to separate himself from the competition with aggressive marketing and advertising strategies that sell homes fast and for more money. Paul's radio show, Open House, the Real Estate & Mortgage Show as well as the Gemini Award nominated network TV show "All For Nothing" are wide reaching and help audiences and people who he normally would be unable to personally help.

18

Finalizing
The Sale

Bruce Hammer
Golden State Realty Group
Sacramento, California

Many different parties are involved in a home purchase. In addition to the buyer and seller, there may be one or more real estate professionals, a loan officer, home inspector, escrow or title officer and/or closing attorney. The happiest moment for all parties is when confirmation is received that the sale has been recorded and escrow is closed. That is the moment when funds are exchanged and title actually transfers from the seller to the buyer. At this moment the new homeowner achieves the American dream of home ownership, the sellers breathe a sigh of relief for having lost the 500 pound mortgage gorilla on their back, and the real estate agents and other professionals involved in the sale are paid – lots of celebrating goes on!

Unfortunately, there is a lot of ground to cover between point A (buyer's offer accepted by seller) and point Z (closing of escrow). Fortunately, most of the professionals involved in your transaction have been through the selling process countless times and know it inside and out, but there are some things that all parties must pay attention to. This chapter will discuss some of those important details.

Timelines in Purchase Agreements

An accepted real estate purchase offer is a binding contract. This means that there are consequences if the terms of the agreement are breached or violated by either party. According to a law known as the "statute of frauds," real estate contracts must be written. This makes it easier to determine the duties of the sellers and buyers, but also makes it easier to determine whether the contract has been breached by one of the parties.

CHAPTER 18 – FINALIZING THE SALE

Transaction Deadlines and Common Benchmarks

Once an offer has been accepted and is executed by both the buyer and seller, the selling process begins. Most real estate contracts require both the buyer and seller to complete certain tasks within specific time periods. The first of these deadlines for the buyers is usually to get their earnest money deposit to the designated escrow company or closing attorney. In some contracts, the earnest money deposit is required within 24 hours, but others allow several days. The timeline depends on the terms agreed upon in the contract.

Although simple to accomplish, the act of turning over the buyer's earnest money to a 3rd party can be a good indicator of how complication-free the rest of the transaction will be. If the contract calls for an escrow company to receive the buyer's earnest money within 72 hours of contract acceptance, the money had better arrive at the escrow company within 72 hours!

Your real estate agent needs to be committed to the transaction and on top of deadlines. They should contact the escrow officer or closing attorney to obtain written confirmation that the earnest money was received as agreed. If it doesn't arrive on time, your agent should immediately contact the buyer's agent. Why is this so critical? First, it sets the stage for the future of the transaction. Secondly, failing to come forward with earnest money could be a signal that the buyer is not motivated to complete the sale.

In recent years, some buyers have made offers on and negotiated the purchase of multiple properties at the same time, even though they will only purchase one. These buyers may have no intention of buying your property; they just want to legally tie up several properties until they begin eliminating those that they don't really want to buy.

Most contracts have a specified inspection period that allows buyers to cancel without the loss of their earnest money if within the number of days specified. The inspection period could be 10 days, 17 days, 21 days, or more. Even though the buyers can cancel without penalty, ensuring that their earnest money is deposited will help weed out the imposters early. It is much better that a deal fall apart after 3 days than 30 days.

Many real estate contracts contain clauses that place time constraints on the buyer to obtain loan approval. They may also have clauses stating that, regardless of the inspection results, the buyer can cancel without penalty if they cannot obtain a loan. Buyers may also be able to cancel the contract if the property doesn't appraise for at least the agreed upon purchase price. These "get out of jail free" provisions are known as "contingencies."

Buyers think of contingencies as a way to "get out of" buying your home. If the appraisal is not as high as their offer price, repair issues are found in the inspection, or the buyer cannot obtain financing, they can usually cancel the contract. If these contingencies are not removed, the buyer's earnest money may be returned to them if the sale fails to close. A good listing agent will ensure that the contingencies are removed by the deadlines provided in the contract.

CHAPTER 18 – FINALIZING THE SALE

Your agent should also be in regular contact with the buyer's agent, the buyer's lender, the escrow/title officer, and possibly the closing attorney. All of these parties play an important role in moving the process from contract to closing. If any of them "drop the ball" by failing to do their job, your sale can fall apart. For example, assume that the preliminary title report lists an unreleased lien on your property which will take an extra 30 days to remove. If the report is not received and read by all parties, everyone will assume that the sale will close on time. A small issue such as this could not only delay closing, it could kill the deal!

The same thing could happen if the buyer's lender drops the ball and forgets to order the appraisal. Unfortunately, these and other issues like them occur every day. An experienced listing agent will be on top of the process to ensure that each party understands the importance of their responsibilities and completes their tasks on time throughout the transaction. Your listing agent is crucial to ensuring that your sale closes on time without unexpected problems.

These are just a few of the many issues your real estate agent must stay on top of during the sale of your home. As illustrated above, a lot of detail—much of it behind the scenes—is involved in getting from contract to closing. An experienced listing agent with a solid record of sales can mean the difference between a jubilant celebration and an emotional roller coaster that ends in heartache. Choose your agent wisely!

About The Author

Bruce Hammer

Golden State Realty Group
3835 N Freeway Blvd. Suite 140
Sacramento, CA 95834

(916) 960-1774

bruce@colemanhammer.com

www.sacramentohousefinder.com

Bruce Hammer was born and raised in the San Francisco Bay Area. After military service, he earned a BS degree from the College of Notre Dame in 1991 and an MBA in 1998. He got his real estate license in 1988 and began managing foreclosures in the loan servicing industry. He acquired, rehabbed, and sold foreclosed properties as an Asset Manager for PMI Mortgage Insurance Company. It was a natural progression to sell traditional and REO listings.

Bruce is co-owner of Golden State Realty Group, Inc., in Sacramento, CA. Bruce's strong work ethic and knowledge of the industry have earned him numerous industry awards and he is consistently ranked in the elite top one half of one percent of all practicing licensees in the Sacramento tri-county area.

Bruce is a member of the National REO Brokers Association, a Certified Distressed Property Expert, Life Member of the Sacramento Association of Realtors® Masters Club, and REO4Kids, a national organization of real estate brokers who support children's charities on every sale.

SUMMARY

We hope the information contained in this book has helped to educate you about the home-selling process and has given you a better idea of questions to ask potential real estate agents before you hire them.

Selling a home is the single largest financial investment most people will make during their lifetime. It is important to find an experienced and ethical real estate agent to assist you. If you don't live in a market area serviced by an author of this book, please contact one of us so we can recommend someone in your area who is qualified to help you sell your home fast and for top dollar with the least amount of hassle.

We've spent many years in real estate coaching with Craig Proctor, who became the number one selling RE/MAX agent in the world at the age of 26 and remained in the top ten for *sixteen years* until retiring in 2009. Craig's Quantum Leap coaching program is the most expensive real estate education in North America. It provides the agents who invest in themselves with the tools, knowledge, and experience to succeed in any market!

Why would you hire anyone who offers less? Our expertise in creative marketing, offer analysis, and skillful negotiation strategies can literally put tens of thousands of dollars in your pocket. Find us! It will be worth the effort!

Happy Home Selling!

CPSIA information can be obtained at www.ICGtesting.com
Printed in the USA
BVOW040641170512

290212BV00003BA/1/P